# INSTANT ITALIAN

# INSTANT ITALIAN

*100 Recipes for Stylish Dishes in Minutes*

**VALENTINA HARRIS**

*Special photography by*
**DAVID GILL**

**CONRAN OCTOPUS**

*For Greg, because you widened my horizons
and made me laugh.*

First published in 1992 by
Conran Octopus Limited
37 Shelton Street
London WC2H 9HN

Reprinted 1993, 1994

This paperback edition published in 1995 by
Conran Octopus Limited

Text copyright © 1992 Valentina Harris
Special photography copyright © 1992 David Gill
Design copyright © 1992 Conran Octopus Limited

The right of Valentina Harris to be identified as the author of this work has been asserted by her in accordance with the Copyright, Designs and Patents Act 1988.

All rights reserved. No part of this work may be reproduced, stored in a retrieval system or transmitted in any form or by any means, electronic, electrostatic, magnetic tape, mechanical, photocopying, recording or otherwise, without the prior permission in writing of the publisher.

Both metric and imperial quantities are given in the recipes. Use either all metric or all imperial, as the two are not interchangeable.

Art Director **Karen Bowen**
Project Editor **Louise Simpson**
Editor **Beverly LeBlanc**
Editorial Assistant **Josephine Mead**
Production **Alison McIver**
Home Economist **Meg Jansz**
Photographic Stylist **Róisín Nield**
Backgrounds **Lynne Robinson and Richard Lowther**

A CIP catalogue record for this book is available from the British Library

ISBN 1 85029 672 3

Typeset by Hunters Armley Limited

Printed in Hong Kong

## CONTENTS

**INTRODUCTION**
6

**PASTA**
*and*
**RISOTTI**
64

**ANTIPASTI**
*and*
**STARTERS**
18

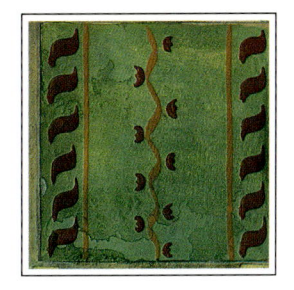

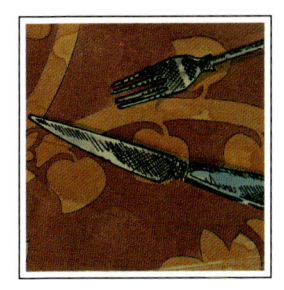

**MEAT**
*and*
**POULTRY**
84

**LIGHT SNACKS**
32

**FISH**
*and*
**SHELLFISH**
98

**SALADS**
48

**FRUIT**
*and*
**DESSERTS**
112

**INDEX**
126

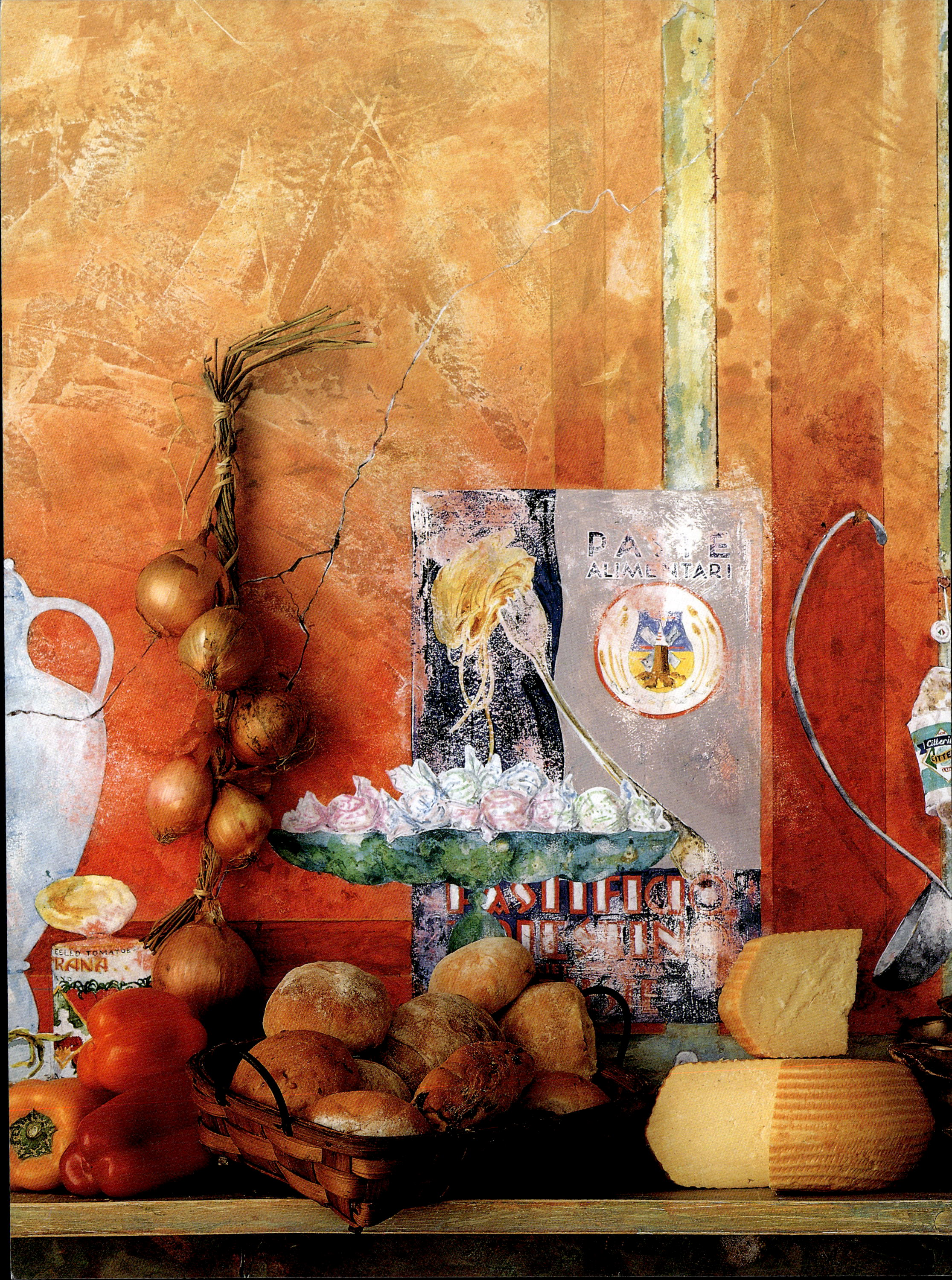
PASTE
ALIMENTARI
PASTIFICIO

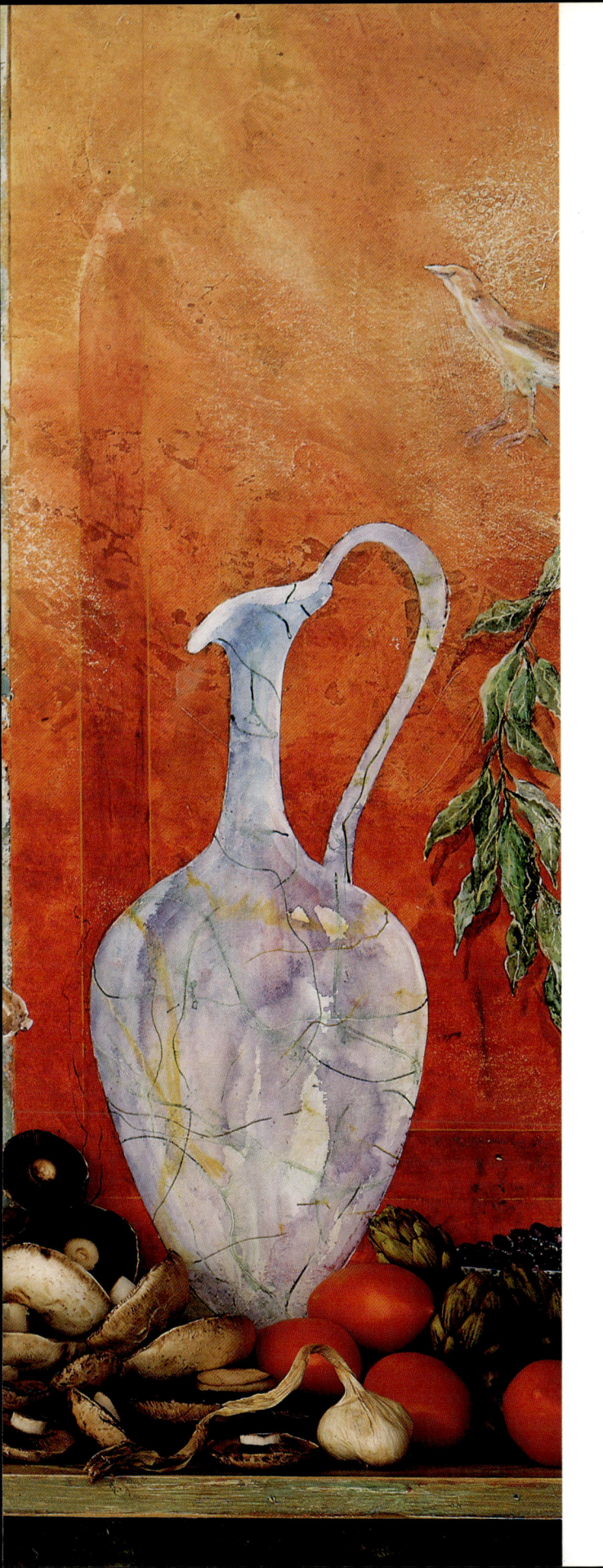

# INTRODUCTION

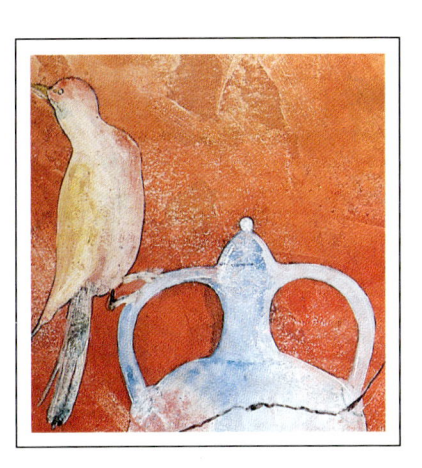

*Italian food is ideally suited to quick cooking. Its basic ingredients have such good, strong flavours and firm textures that you can create colourful, gutsy dishes, which are authentically Italian, in minutes.*

Today in Italy, life has become far too hectic for many families to spend hours preparing a meal. Lighter, healthier dishes are often preferred to hearty sauces, stews and soups, especially in northern Italy, and chic restaurants have introduced marvellously light, inviting dishes. In fact, it is becoming more and more rare, particularly among the younger generation, for cooks to go to the kind of lengthy preparation I recall happening in the kitchen at home. But this doesn't for one moment mean Italy has lost her passion for good food. Far from it. The same degree of passion exists now, as it always has done. The only difference now is that cooks are experimenting and discovering ways of retaining this great love for cooking and eating delicious food, but in a way which takes less of their valuable time.

This is the ultimate book for all who adore Italian food, but have very little spare time to indulge in their love of cooking. In this collection of recipes you will find nothing that takes longer than 35 minutes to prepare from start to finish – with most taking less than 25 minutes.

A well-stocked store cupboard with tins of basic ingredients and jars containing items which are a bit more luxurious, means you can quickly put together a range of dishes with a minimum of fuss. Whenever I see something a bit unusual at a delicatessen which will keep well for some time, I buy it and tuck it at the back of my cupboard. Sooner or later, in my experience, it comes in very useful, whether it is a jar of creamy walnut sauce for pasta, or some cherries preserved in brandy, delicious with ice cream.

# INGREDIENTS

**BREAD** Bread makes a very good base for lots of quick-and-easy dishes. As with all other dishes that require very little cooking, however, it is important that the bread should have a good flavour and texture to begin with. Ciabatta bread is currently the most widely available and most popular variety of Italian bread sold by supermarkets, but there are many others. Olive bread is delicious with thinly sliced prosciutto or cheese. Walnut bread is also very good with cheese, especially Parmesan or Taleggio. If you can't find ciabatta bread, which is required for several of the recipes in this book, really good quality French baguettes are a passable alternative.

**MEAT AND CURED MEATS** As far as fresh meat is concerned, to cook it quickly, you'll need the more tender and expensive cuts. They will also tend to be well trimmed and require less time to prepare.

Look for any of these cuts: minute steaks, fillet steaks, pork loin (cut into thin strips), veal escalopes, turkey escalopes, chicken breasts, lamb noisettes, lamb cutlets, thinly cut sirloin steaks and duck breasts. Whatever cut you buy, please remember to go for top-quality meat. It is far better to serve small quantities of really tasty, tender meat rather than large quantities of something chewy and inferior.

Calf's liver is also very quick to cook and is extremely tender and delicious. Seal it quickly in a frying pan in piping hot butter or olive oil on either side until it goes dark brown, leaving the inside moist and pink. The most classical dish is *fegato alla Veneziana*, pan-fried calf's liver served on a bed of caramelized onions.

Prosciutto crudo is probably the best known of all the cured meats. It is usually labelled just as 'prosciutto' or called Parma ham, although real Parma ham only comes from the Langhirano valley near Parma. Prosciutto crudo, which is cured and salted raw ham, is made all over Italy and many different types are available. Parma ham remains arguably the best, although I am especially partial to San Daniele ham, from the very top north-eastern corner of the country.

There are always lots of different kinds of salame available in a good delicatessen. Here are four of the better-known varieties: Finocchiona, a big, very hearty salame peppered with fennel seeds; Milano, a fairly fine-grained salame with a mild flavour; Napoletano, a fiery salame tinged with red due to the chilli mixed into the meat; and Felino, a thin, soft little salame with a very meaty flavour.

Other cured meats include pancetta, coppa, mortadella, culatello, speck, lonza and bresaola. Of all these, only bresaola is not made with pork. Bresaola is cured air-dried beef fillet which is sold in very thin slices and is normally served with a sprinkling of olive oil, lemon juice and freshly milled black pepper. Pancetta is cured belly of pork, and can sometimes be extremely highly seasoned with pepper and rosemary as well as salt. It is ideal if you require a really strong bacon flavour, but I would not recommend that you eat it raw. If you can't find Italian bacon, a quality, full-flavoured streaky bacon is perfectly acceptable.

**FISH AND SEAFOOD** Fish is easy and quick to cook as long as it is fresh, firm fleshed and carefully prepared by a fishmonger. Ready-prepared portions of fresh fish from supermarkets are expensive, but they are very convenient.

Fillets of sole and plaice and monkfish tails all have firm textures and their relatively delicate flavours make them ideal to combine with other ingredients. Trout and salmon are also extremely quick to cook. Using salmon steaks or salmon tails is a very fast and easy way of preparing impressive dishes.

Seafood is good in fast dishes as it also doesn't need much cooking. Buy squid already cleaned and sliced into rings, or as hollow cylinders for stuffing and baking. Mussels are very quick, too, although they need a thorough cleaning first. Try to buy raw prawns and simply brush with olive oil, push them on to skewers and then grill until pink and juicy.

**VEGETABLES AND SALADS** Fresh tomatoes, sweet juicy peppers in a variety of colours, aubergines, courgettes, fennel, spinach, swiss chard, rocket and radicchio are all vegetables which typify Italian cookery, and most of them are available at supermarkets all year round. Naturally, all of them will be cheapest and at their peak when they are in season, and there is no doubt in my mind that the organically grown varieties taste much better even though they are more expensive. Rocket, a delicious pungent herb, can be grown from seed in your garden and used in salads and soups.

Whatever kind of vegetable you are cooking, remember to cook it only for the briefest possible time to retain all it's flavour, crunchiness, vitamins and colour. If you are using vegetables like broccoli, cauliflower or cabbage, remember to break them into very small florets or to shred the leaves very finely so they cook in just a few minutes.

In a traditional Italian mixed salad, *insalata mista*, you will probably find shredded carrots, finely chopped onions, sliced cucumbers, sliced tomatoes and chopped celery, as well as several different kinds of salad leaves.

**FRUIT** Fresh fruit is a perfect and speedy dessert. Try strawberries, raspberries and sliced peaches with white wine, or apricots with ricotta cheese and walnuts, and mascarpone cheese is perfect with ripe pears. Parma ham is famous for its partnership with melon, but it is also superb with papaya, mango, figs, avocados, kiwis and pears. Salame is also excellent with fresh figs, and goats' cheese and grapes make a very simple and delightful antipasto.

**MUSHROOMS** The Italian passion for mushrooms is legendary. Every year hundreds of families spend many happy hours gathering wild mushrooms of all kinds in the forests and woods of Italy. I am much too nervous to gather wild mushrooms without a bona fide expert present, so I shall not attempt to advise you! Fortunately, most greengrocers and supermarkets now sell a variety of mushrooms with different flavours, colours and shapes, all of which make it much easier for me to enjoy mushrooms without the worries of mispicking. Brown caps, oyster, shiitake and field mushrooms are now available at most supermarkets alongside the more usual variety of mushroom in all different sizes.

Italian porcini mushrooms are very rarely available for sale fresh in this country. Buy them dried, and pre-soak them for about 10 minutes before adding to a dish, straining the mushrooms first to avoid bits of wood or earth in your dish. I like to combine a few dried mushrooms with some fresh cultivated mushrooms to give recipes a really punchy flavour.

**CHEESE** In my opinion, Italian cheeses are second to none and can easily hold their own with the very best that any major cheese producing country offers. The king of Italian cheeses has to be *Parmigiano Reggiano*. Parmesan has become the generic term for all Italian hard grating cheese, but, in fact, there are three distinctive types of hard grating cheese. All three have a similar texture, but vary a great deal in flavour and quality. Top of the list is *Parmigiano*, followed by *Grana Padano* and then *Grana Trentino*. Each can be used in cooking or eaten on its own. When you do eat them on their own, remember that the younger the cheese, the softer and sweeter it tastes.

Other easily available Italian cheeses that supermarkets, as well as delicatessens stock, include: ricotta, a creamy white cheese used a great deal in both savoury and sweet cooking; mozzarella, a white, round, slicing cheese that is very good for cooking purposes but is also useful in salads if it is very fresh; Gorgonzola, an old-fashioned blue cheese from Lombardy with the texture of ripe brie – it can be very piquant or quite mild depending on the variety;

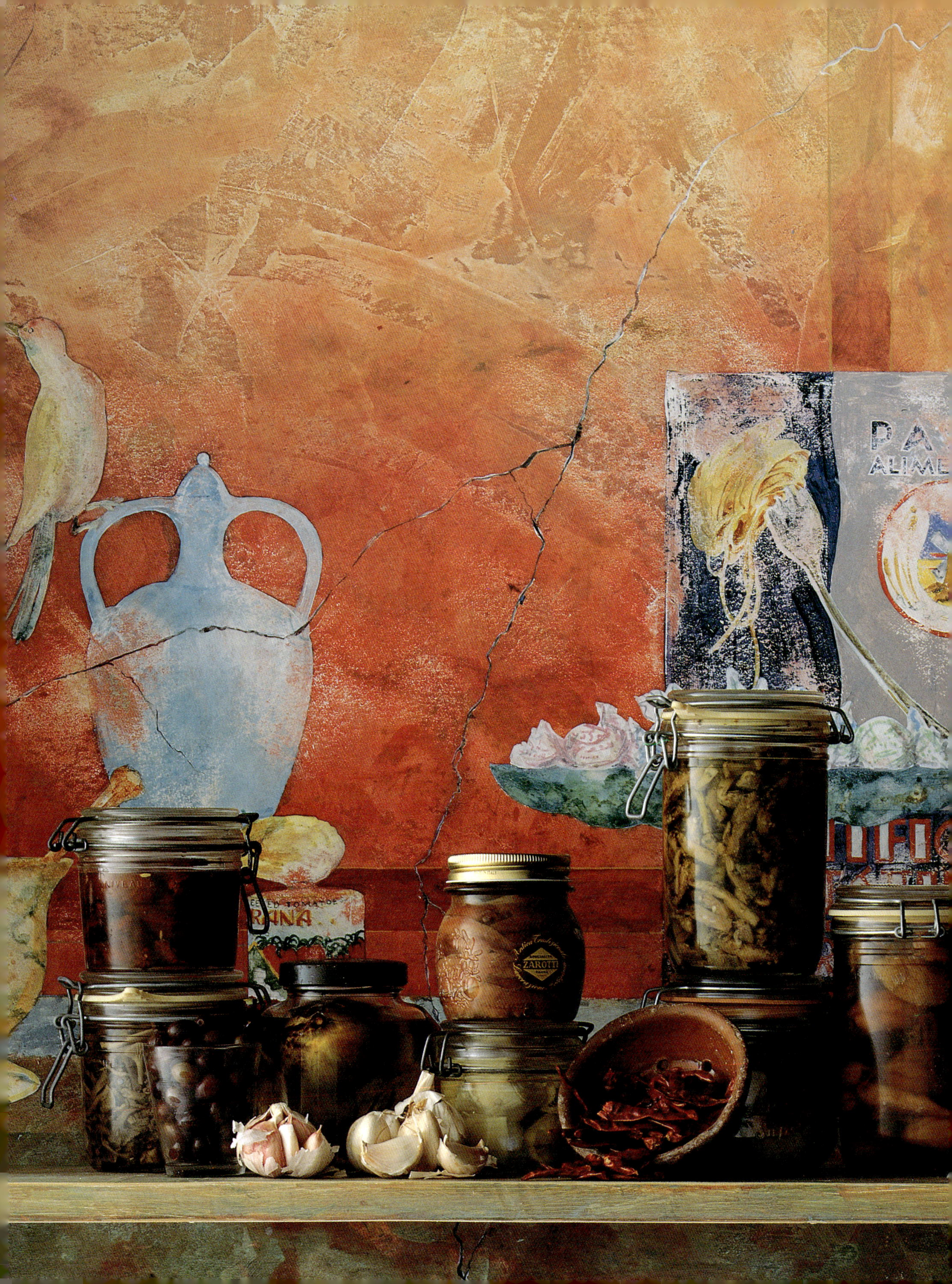
ZAROTTI

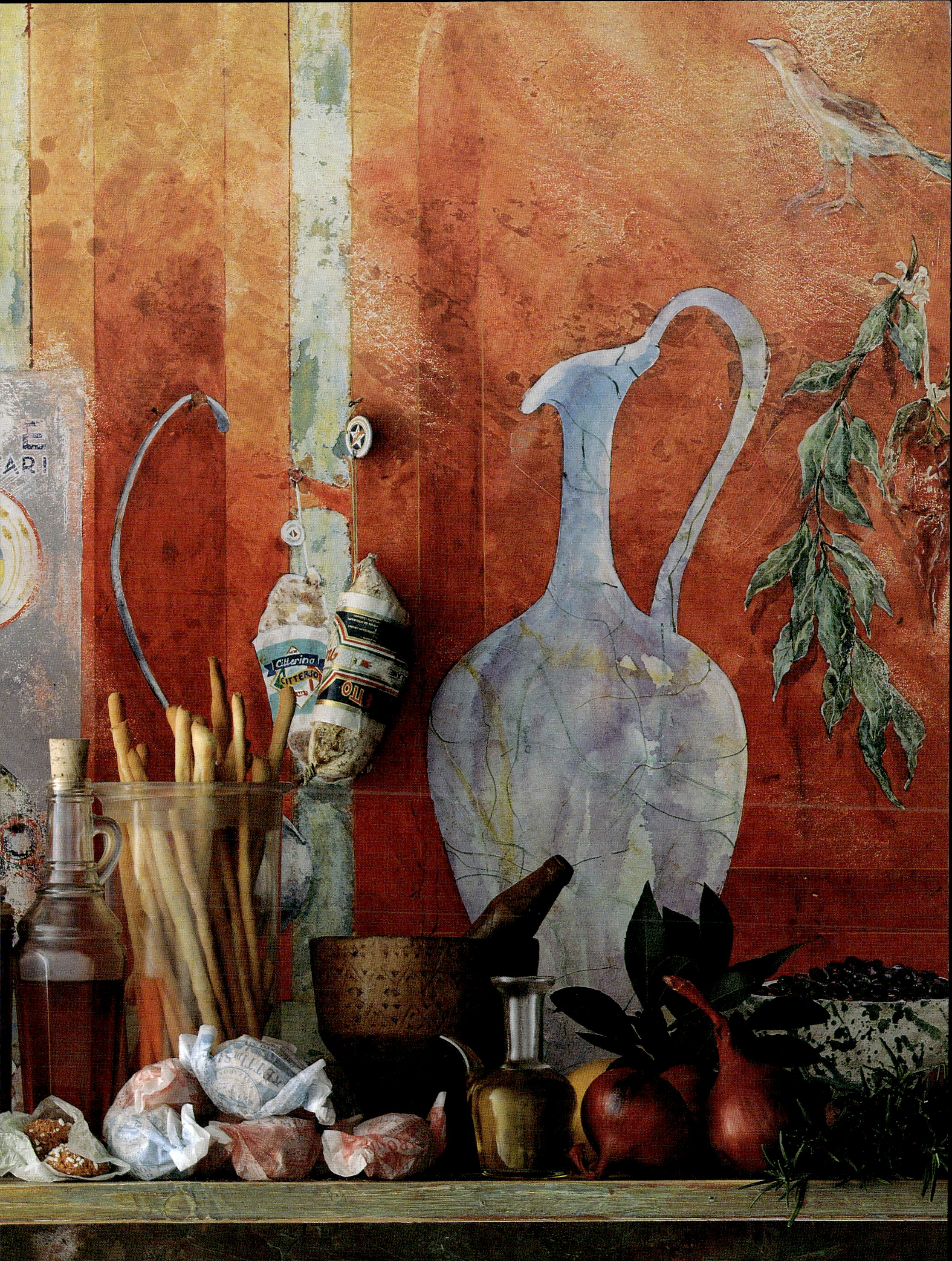
Citterina
CITTERIO

mascarpone, which is much more like clotted cream than cheese and is used in cooking – absolutely delectable with soft ripe pears.

Caprino is a very mild white, tube-shaped goats' cheese sold wrapped individually in paper squares. Sometimes it is preserved in olive oil and black peppercorns. Pecorino is a hard ewes' milk cheese that is made all over southern Italy and is sold in varying stages of piquancy. It can be grated over pasta or eaten on it's own.

**SEA SALT AND BLACK PEPPER** In Italian households you will find two varieties of salt – *sale grosso* and *sale fino*. The former is coarse-grain sea salt, which is ideal for adding to water which is to be used for boiling pasta or vegetables. The latter is fine grained for sprinkling into a dish. Although not typically Italian, ground black pepper is now a feature of Italian cooking, and I recommend freshly milled black pepper for a full flavour.

**ONIONS** Lightly fried in oil or butter, onions form the basis of many dishes. I like to use both sweet red onions and stronger more piquant brown onions.

**DRIED RED CHILLI PEPPERS** No Italian kitchen would be complete without at least one jar of dried red chillis. I like to have bunches of them hanging from the ceiling, so I either grow a few plants myself if the summer is hot enough and then dry them, or I bury ready-made bunches of them in my luggage on each visit home.

You can buy ready-made chilli oil, which is even quicker to use, and tastes more fiery than the oil you'll make at home, although home-made chilli oil gets stronger as it matures. Chillis also come in a finely ground powder, which is easy to sprinkle into food, or more coarsely ground with a much rougher texture.

To release the natural oils from dried chillis quickly, rub them lightly in the palms of your hands for just a few seconds. The heat from your hands will help the chilli to 'sweat' slightly. But please wash your hands immediately after doing this, and do not touch your eyes or your lips until you have done so. Also, please keep chillis, chilli powder, crushed chillis and chilli oil out of the reach of small children at all times.

**GARLIC** In my opinion, fresh garlic in a bulb is the only garlic worth considering. I don't like garlic salt, and I have yet to find a type of garlic purée worth buying. When I do have time, I crush about 20 peeled cloves of garlic together in the food processor, then keep the resulting purée in a screw-top jar in the fridge, to use as required.

**HERBS** Italian cooking relies a great deal upon the use of herbs. With some notable exceptions, it is always preferable to use fresh herbs as they give a much truer flavour than the dried varieties. I like to use freeze-dried herbs when I can't have fresh herbs because they have a much brighter colour and a more intense taste. When you do use dried herbs, however, you'll need to use less than the fresh variety, because the drying process always intensifies the flavour.

Some supermarkets and greengrocers sell small pots of growing herbs such as parsley, basil and chives. These are quite good value because they last longer than a packet of freshly cut herbs and cost about the same. Fresh cut herbs keep very well in the fridge in a green 'stay fresh' bag, available from all good health food shops. Alternatively, you can keep them wrapped in damp newspaper.

The herbs used most commonly in Italian cookery are: rosemary, mint, basil, sage, parsley, oregano, thyme, marjoram and bay leaves. Of these, basil and parsley really *must* be used as fresh herbs, whereas oregano only really comes into its own when it is dried.

With other fresh herbs, you can chop handfuls of them when they are at their peak and freeze them in small quantities to use straight from the freezer.

**SAFFRON** In Italy, saffron is always sold and used in tiny little rectangular sachets not in threads. In just 20 minutes, you can create a rich golden risotto with one tiny sachet of this precious spice, some rice, butter, onion and well-flavoured stock.

**STOCKS** Stock is an essential element in all good cooking, however it does take quite a long time to make it properly. The best thing to do is to make it when you do have time and then freeze it. Make sure you make different kinds of stock – meat, chicken, vegetable and fish – so you always have what you require. It is not a good idea to freeze stock in large amounts because it is unlikely you'll need so much all in one go. It is far better to reduce it down, then pour it into an ice-cube tray, freeze it in cubes and then store the cubes in clearly-labelled plastic bags.

If you don't want to make your own stock, or you happen to have run out, you can now buy excellent ready-made stocks in a liquid jelly-like form. These are fresh, so they can easily be frozen.

Italian home cooks have no qualms at all about adding stock cubes to their cooking, although they never add a whole cube. Usually a small piece of cube is considered sufficient to add the required amount of flavour. The main thing about stock cubes is that most of them contain a great deal of salt, so you should be careful how you use them. Concentrated stocks in tubs or bottles are being improved all the time, but I must stress that you should be careful how much you add to a dish to avoid oversalting.

**OILS** Olive oil is perhaps the most important ingredient for authentic Italian cookery. Extra-virgin olive oil means it comes from the first pressing. It is oil that contains the lowest level of oleic acid and, therefore, has the most rounded flavour. It is purer and more expensive than virgin olive oil, which is oil of the second pressing. Oil which is simply called 'olive oil' refers to pressings made thereafter. The final product is called sansa oil and is made from whatever is left after the very final pressing.

In order of quality, extra-virgin is the top of the range. It has the most intense flavour, so it is best used for salads, or where very small quantities of oil are required. Virgin oil has a less intense flavour and can therefore be freely used for both salads and for cooking. Olive oil has a very mild flavour and is best used just for cooking. Sansa oil is not generally sold for domestic use but is used commercially for deep-frying. I think that sunflower oil is best used for deep-frying, however, as it gives an even, golden colouring and has a mild enough flavour not to overpower the taste of what you are frying. It also has a very low saturated fat content.

**PINE NUTS, ALMONDS AND OTHER NUTS**
Although pine nuts tend to be rather expensive, adding a few to a dish instantly adds not only the inimitable flavour of this resinous nut, but also a marvellously crunchy texture. You can add them to salads, to pasta sauces, to soups or to fish or meat dishes. In desserts, you can sprinkle them into a fruit salad or on top of a cake, or even add them to ice cream. They are a very versatile and an easy to use ingredient, and they are typical of Italian cooking.

Though they are not as widely used in Italy, shelled walnuts, shelled hazelnuts and blanched almonds are also very good standbys and can be added to a wide variety of dishes for instant flavour and texture.

**VINEGAR** I think malt vinegars tend to be so very sharp that they destroy the flavour of a dish. I like to use red or white wine vinegars at all times, both for cooking and for salad dressings. I also like to have a bottle of balsamic vinegar in my store cupboard because it is a very quick way of adding an exotic hint of flavour to even the blandest dish. Whilst true balsamic comes only from Modena and is very expensive, there is a younger commercial variety which is perfectly acceptable for use and is on sale in many supermarkets and delicatessens. Just a few drops of balsamic vinegar add a delicious sweet-and-sour flavour to a salad dressing. You can also sprinkle a few drops on to a steak as it grills, or add a little to cured meats or on to steamed or poached fish. Always use it sparingly.

**ANCHOVIES** The use of anchovies in Italian cookery imparts a very strong and intense flavour to many dishes. It is very quick and simple to start off a sauce for pasta by melting down anchovy fillets in olive oil and garlic to make a creamy brown base. The very strong taste of the anchovy gives any dish an immediate burst of flavour. I prefer to use salted anchovies, which need to be carefully boned, washed and dried before use, because they melt down much better than the kind preserved in oil and also have a stronger flavour. Tubed anchovy paste is also useful.

**FRESH PASTA AND READY-MADE SAUCES**
Hand-made or machine-made fresh pasta cooks extremely quickly. Fresh tagliatelle, for example, only needs 3 or 4 minutes before it is drained and dressed with a sauce of your choice, compared to dried durum wheat spaghetti which needs about 7 minutes to cook.

Making fresh pasta from scratch requires both time and expertise, but fortunately you can now buy ready-made fresh pasta from supermarkets and delicatessens. You can also buy fresh dried pasta (i.e. pasta made with eggs and flour) called *pasta all'uovo*. This is also very quick to cook and, although brands vary enormously in quality, it can be delicious and taste just like proper fresh pasta.

Many shops also sell ready-made tortellini and

ravioli, which consist of pockets of fresh pasta with a filling inside them. These vary enormously in quality, but once you find a brand that you like, they make a very quick and easy meal. For example, tortellini with a spinach and ricotta cheese stuffing only need to be boiled, drained and dressed with melted butter flavoured with sage and freshly grated Parmesan.

As far as the sauces are concerned, I always avoid using ready-made sauces in jars because they seem to have a very artificial aftertaste and they never taste anywhere near like the home-made version.

Frankly, you can make a sauce for your pasta in the same amount of time that it takes to bring the water to the boil and cook the pasta itself, so I really don't see the point of spending money on a ready-made sauce when you can do so much better yourself. A very quick favourite in my house is pasta with an avocado purée flavoured with a little garlic, some chopped fresh parsley, a few spoonfuls of natural yogurt and a handful of grated Parmesan cheese. All the ingredients for the sauce can be whizzed in the food processor while the pasta is boiling, after which all you have to do is drain the pasta and mix it with the sauce. *Ecco Fatto!*

**DRIED DURUM WHEAT PASTA** A few packets of dried durum wheat pasta in a varied selection of shapes is the best possible standby ingredient. Depending upon the shape you choose to buy, it will take more or less time to actually cook.

There are a few basic points about cooking pasta, whether it be fresh or dried, which really must be respected if you want to achieve good results.
1 Use a really BIG saucepan. The more space pasta has to move around in, the better texture it will have. If you have a big enough saucepan with enough space, you will never need to add oil to the water to prevent the pasta sticking to itself as it cooks.
2 Make sure the water is REALLY boiling before you add the pasta, or it may stick together. It does not matter when you add the salt but it is vital that the water must be at a rolling boil before you add the pasta to the pan.
3 Stir the pasta frequently as it cooks.
4 Drain the pasta immediately it is cooked. The best way to know if pasta is cooked is to fish out a piece and taste it. If you consider it 'done', drain it immediately. Generally speaking, pasta needs to be drained very thoroughly to remove any excess water.

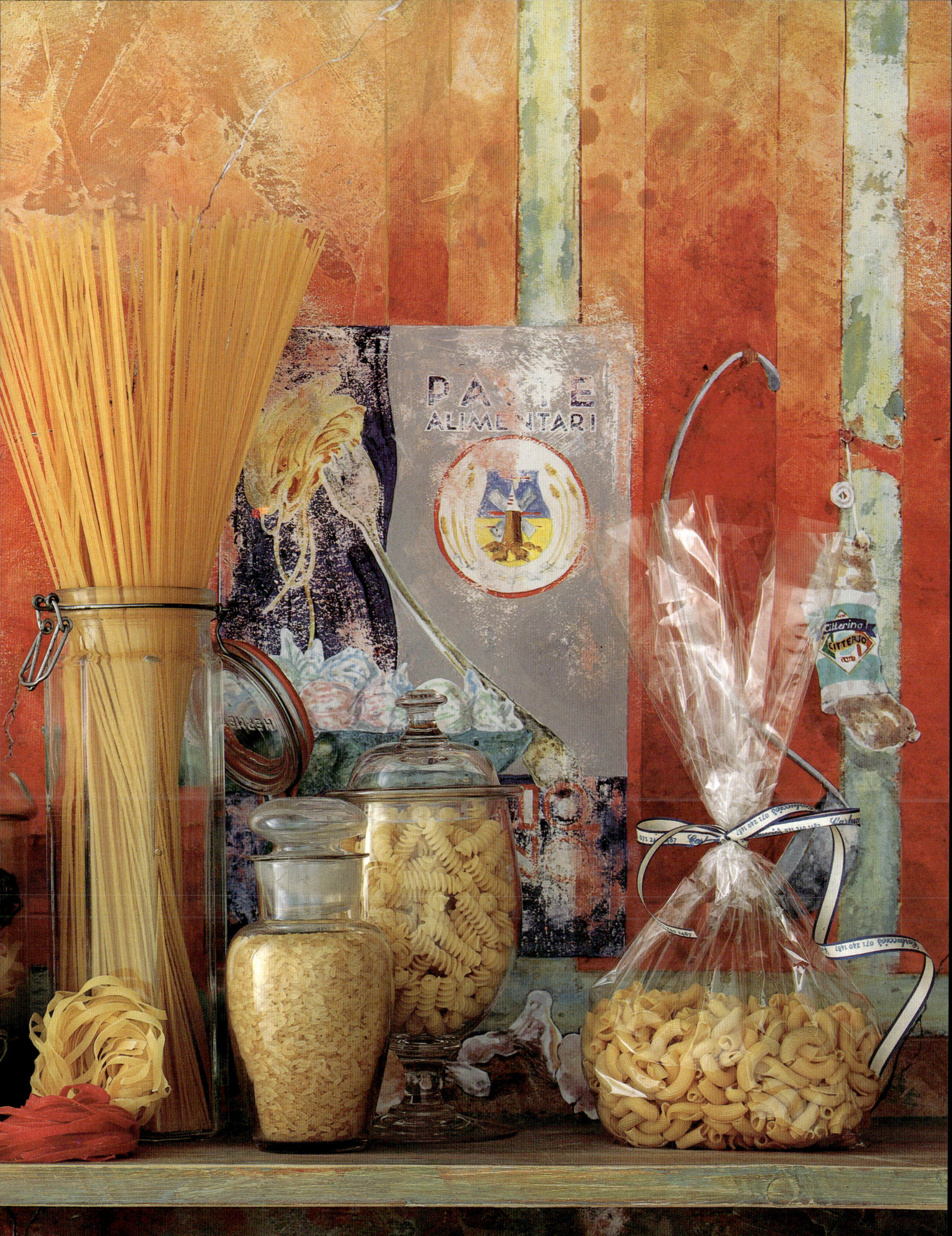
PASTE
ALIMENTARI

and remember that whatever water you leave in the pasta will only dilute your sauce. For creamy sauces, however, it is often better to leave a tiny amount of water (2 to 3 tablespoons) to help the sauce distribute itself amongst the pasta more easily.

**5** Act quickly once you have drained the pasta to prevent it cooling and also because it will continue to cook for as long as it is sitting around. Return it to the saucepan, add the sauce, mix together and transfer to a serving dish or on to plates.

The other aspect about pasta which needs some consideration is which shape of pasta to use with which sauce. This is largely down to personal preference and availability, although certain sauces marry best with certain shapes. As a general rule, chunky, short shapes are best with chunky sauces, and the more delicate shapes go better with the lighter, more delicate sauces. However, there is absolutely nothing to stop you using whatever is in your cupboard at the time!

**RICE AND RISOTTO** There is no getting away from it – a proper risotto takes 20-30 minutes from the time you begin cooking it. The reason is the rice. You must use risotto rice to get the right texture and flavour. If you use any other rice, such as long grain rice, quick rice, pudding rice, brown rice or basmati rice, you will not end up with an authentic Italian risotto. Fortunately, risotto rice is now readily available at most supermarkets.

**PESTO** Various brands are now available in this country, so experiment with a few until you find the one you like best. Pesto is a combination of fresh basil with pine kernels, Parmesan cheese, garlic and olive oil. It is wonderful on freshly boiled and drained pasta, stirred into soups, brushed on to fish before grilling or spread on to bread as a sandwich base. It adds the superbly strident flavour of an Italian summer. If a dish calls for fresh basil but you can't get hold of it, a spoonful of pesto is much better than dried basil.

**CANNED TOMATOES** An essential standby for sauces and crostini topping, but always cook first.

**PASSATA** Passata consists of nothing more complicated than canned plum tomatoes which have been sieved for you, removing all seeds and lumps. It is much easier than using plum tomatoes as it cooks quicker and smoothly mixes into other ingredients. It is sold in cartons or glass jars and only costs a little more than ordinary canned tomatoes.

**INGREDIENTS PRESERVED IN OLIVE OIL** All manner of ingredients can be preserved in olive oil, from tiny little sausages to artichoke hearts and mushrooms. You can buy jars of these various ingredients at supermarkets and more especially at delicatessens. Many of them are particularly good to add to a dish of thinly sliced cured meats as part of an antipasto. Others, such as sun-dried tomatoes, olives or dried chillis preserved in olive oil can be added to sauces for pasta or used as part of a salad.

**SUN-DRIED TOMATOES** These are much cheaper if you buy them dry as opposed to preserved in olive oil. When you have more time on your hands to spend in the kitchen, I recommend you soak the dried tomatoes in milk overnight, then drain and rinse them thoroughly. Arrange them in layers in a jar, covering each layer generously with olive oil until you have filled the jar.

**BEANS, LENTILS AND CHICK-PEAS** All kinds of beans are available in cans, and I like to have as many different varieties as possible to hand for soups and salads: butter beans, borlotti beans, cannellini beans, haricot beans, kidney beans and pinto beans.

The humble chick-pea is equally at home in soups, in pasta sauces or in salads, and is easily whizzed in the food processor with olive oil and garlic to make a creamy sauce to spread on to lightly toasted bread or to pour over freshly boiled and drained pasta. Most varieties of dried lentils cook so quickly that there is hardly any need to resort to using canned ones. If using canned lentils, however, make sure you rinse them carefully before use.

**CAPERS** These tiny little green berries are a very quick-and-easy way of adding a good strong, tangy flavour to a dish. If preserved in salt they need very thorough rinsing and drying but if in brine, they can be used directly from the jar. They are often combined with olives, anchovies and tomatoes to make a very gutsy, strongly flavoured sauce for pasta, but they can also be used in any recipe where you want to add a subtly sour flavour without overpowering the dish.

# EQUIPMENT AND TECHNIQUES

**EQUIPMENT** The most important piece of equipment you will ever require in the kitchen is a good knife. This requires a small investment, because really good knives are not cheap, but the money you spend will mean you have a tool which is reliable and very versatile, cutting down on time and making everything much easier. A large, wide-bladed knife can be used for chopping and slicing. A smaller knife is perfect for paring, peeling and trimming.

A strong, sharp pair of scissors is also a worthwhile investment. Scissors make it much easier to cut meat or fish into strips, or to snip herbs and vegetables into small pieces.

A very traditional and extremely useful piece of Italian kitchen equipment is the mezzaluna, or rocking chopper. This is a crescent-shaped blade with a handle on each end. By gripping the handles firmly, you can finely chop herbs, garlic, onions or anything else, using a rhythmic rocking motion.

The food processor has been a very welcome addition to my kitchen. It cuts down enormously on time, and makes all kinds of procedures possible. A food processor means you can make a soup or a smooth sauce in minutes. You can chop, shred and slice more finely and more quickly than ever before.

Other utensils that are bound to save you time and frustration are a very big saucepan for cooking pasta, a metal colander that is big enough to take large quantities of pasta comfortably but that can also be used for cleaning and preparing vegetables, and will double up as a steamer if you have a tight fitting lid.

A saucepan with a heavy base is also important for the even distribution of heat when you cook dishes like risotto, soup or sauces. A frying pan with a heavy base is also important, and I think a good-quality non-stick pan saves an awful lot of time.

**TECHNIQUES** There are certain techniques which are to be avoided if your aim is to cook quickly. Slow braising, simmering, roasting, marinating and stewing all require plenty of time. This immediately excludes quite a few of the more classical Italian specialities. Baked lasagne, for example, needs several hours worth of preparation and baking, and should therefore be saved for a time when you can linger.

This leaves a whole range of other techniques that are perfect for quick cooking. Grilling is one of the fastest and easiest ways of cooking meat, fish and vegetables. Always make sure the grill is preheated for best results, and line your grill pan with foil to keep it clean and save all the juices which may drain out of the ingredients as they cook.

Frying is also very quick and extremely simple. The frying pan needs to be the right size for whatever you are going to put into it and it needs to be preheated before using.

Boiling is fine for pasta, potatoes or other ingredients which can take intensive, hard cooking. For more delicate ingredients such as fish, however, you must opt for poaching. This means a very gentle technique, the water should be hardly moving, but it can be flavoured with herbs, wine or other seasonings to add flavour rather than boil it out.

Searing involves using very intense heat to simply seal meat or certain types of fish on the outside until it is almost charred, leaving the inside juicy and tender but barely cooked. This is done most easily in a frying pan or a skillet. It is best used with specific kinds of meat such as fillet steak, calf's liver, lamb chops or steaks, or salmon, all of which don't need to be cooked right through like poultry or pork.

To enhance all these quick cooking techniques, you need to adopt a few more standard practices which save time and effort, but in exchange give your dishes lots of flavour and a good texture. Unless you are cooking a thick piece of meat and you want the middle to be rare and juicy, it is always best to flatten meat before cooking it. To do this you need a meat mallet or a rolling pin, and a plastic bag. Lay the meat on a board, cover with the plastic bag (not cling film) and beat the meat firmly and evenly on one side. Remove the bag, turn over the meat and repeat. This technique will ensure that the meat is very tender, but also, because it is very thin, it will cook extremely quickly.

It is also a good idea to use a pastry brush for painting your ingredients with oil, melted butter or a sauce before and during the cooking process. This adds flavour and above all, helps to keep ingredients moist and deliciously succulent.

**NOTE** All recipes serve 4, unless otherwise stated. All eggs are size 2 and spoon measures are assumed to be level.

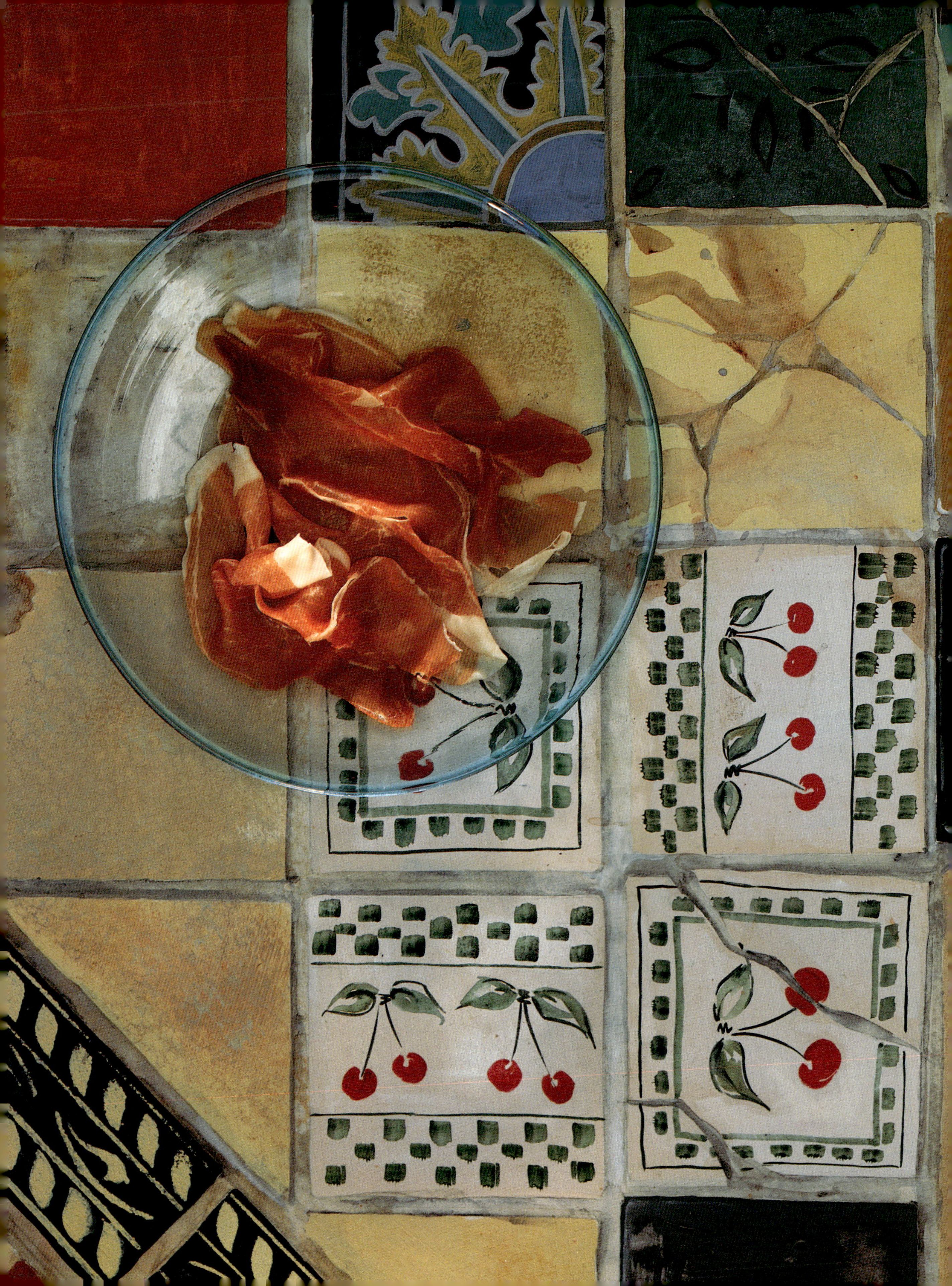

# ANTIPASTI
*and*
# STARTERS

*Traditionally, antipasti are small, tasty snacks, eaten in Italy before the main evening meal, and accompanied by a glass of chilled dry white wine.*

## BRESAOLA WITH SPRING ONIONS
### BRESAOLA CON LA CIPOLLINA

*This is what I call a serious antipasto, because it really needs to be eaten whilst seated at the table, with a knife and fork and plenty of crusty bread. There is no other cured meat in Italy that can be enjoyed dressed in this way, partly because most cured meats are made with pork and bresaola consists of cured fillet of beef. If you serve bresaola with a big green salad and a basket of bread, it becomes a whole meal.*

**TIME 20 MINUTES**

**200 g/7 oz bresaola, thinly sliced**
**juice of ½ lemon, strained**
**5 spring onions, very finely chopped**
**freshly milled black pepper**
**olive oil**
**wedges of lemon, to serve**

**1** Arrange the meat with each slice slightly overlapping to form a single layer on a wide platter.

**2** Sprinkle with the lemon juice, then scatter the spring onions on top and press down firmly with the back of the spoon to release some of the juices.

**3** Grind plenty of black pepper over the meat and then finish with a little (or a lot) of olive oil to taste. Leave to stand for 10 minutes before serving, this is very important in order to let the flavours develop.

**4** Serve with wedges of lemon so that people can squeeze some more juice over their bresaola.

## RICOTTA-STUFFED DATES
### DATTERI RIPIENI DI RICOTTA

*An unusual combination of flavours, but it does in fact work surprisingly well and is delicious with a glass of ice-cold dessert wine, such as Vernaccia.*

**TIME 15 MINUTES • MAKES 20**

**20 large dates**
**20 blanched almonds**
**4 tablespoons fresh ricotta cheese**
**100 g/4 oz sliced pancetta or streaky bacon, rinded if necessary and cut into strips long enough to wrap around the dates**
**2 eggs, beaten**
**3 tablespoons dry white breadcrumbs**
**oil for deep-frying (sunflower or rapeseed)**
**salt**

**1** Slash open the dates and remove the stones.

**2** Replace each stone with a blanched almond, then surround the almond with ricotta, using your fingers and a small spoon. Wrap each date in a small strip of pancetta.

**3** Heat the oil until a small piece of bread dropped into the oil sizzles instantly. Dip the stuffed and wrapped dates in the beaten egg, then roll them in breadcrumbs.

**4** Fry for about 2 minutes, until crispy and golden brown. Drain very thoroughly on kitchen paper and sprinkle with salt. Serve immediately.

*Ricotta-stuffed dates*

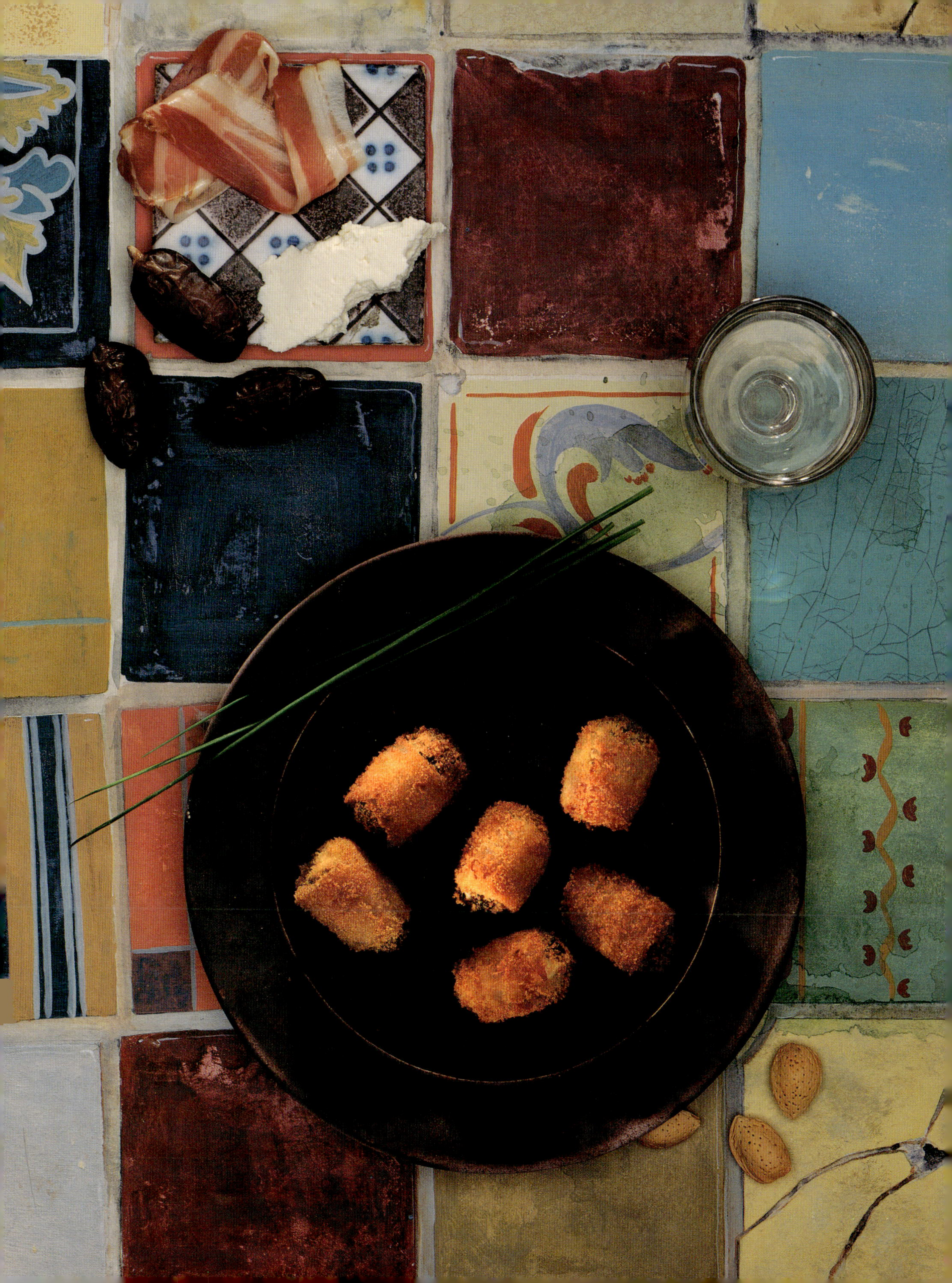

## VARIOUS MINI CROSTINI
### VARI CROSTINI

*These toasted bread slices with an infinite number of possible toppings have recently become very fashionable for serving at parties. My family and I have been eating crostini as snacks or light antipasti for many years, and I am delighted to give you a few of our family favourites. You should be able to find ciabatta bread, a country-style olive oil loaf, in large supermarkets, but if not, use diagonal slices of baguette.*

## MUSHROOM CROSTINI
### CROSTINI AL FUNGHI

TIME 15 MINUTES • MAKES 8

**200 g/7 oz assorted mushrooms, e.g. brown cap, shiitake, oyster, field and wild, cleaned and finely sliced**
**3 tablespoons butter**
**4 tablespoons dry white wine**
**salt and freshly milled black pepper**
**1 heaped tablespoon chopped fresh parsley**
**8 slices of ciabatta bread**
**1 garlic clove, peeled**

**1** Fry the mushrooms with the butter in a wide frying pan, stirring frequently, for about 8 minutes or until softened.

**2** Add the wine and burn off the alcohol, then season and sprinkle with the parsley. Cover the pan and keep warm. Meanwhile, preheat the grill.

**3** Toast the bread lightly on both sides and rub one side with the clove of garlic.

**4** Arrange all the toasted bread on a serving dish. Cover each slice of bread with mushrooms and serve at once.

## CROSTINI WITH CHICKEN LIVERS
### CROSTINI DI FEGATINI

TIME 20 MINUTES • MAKES 24

**2 tablespoons butter**
**120 g/4½ oz onion, chopped**
**250 g/8 oz chicken or turkey livers, well trimmed and rinsed, then quartered**
**1 wine glass dry white wine or Vin Santo**
**salt and freshly milled black pepper**
**1 heaped teaspoon anchovy paste**
**2 tablespoons salted capers, rinsed and dried**
**4 tablespoons chicken stock**
**12 thin slices ciabatta bread, toasted lightly**

**1** Melt the butter in a large frying pan, then fry the onion for about 5 minutes, until softened.

**2** Add the chicken livers and fry them for about 5 minutes, until browned on the outside but still pink in the centre, stirring frequently. Lower the heat slightly, then gradually stir in the wine, allowing it to evaporate between each addition. Season generously with salt and pepper and once all the wine has been added, take the pan off the heat. Leave aside.

**3** Put the chicken livers into the food processor with the anchovy paste and capers. Whizz for just long enough to blend the ingredients, but do not make a smooth purée.

**4** Return to the pan and warm through very gently for about 2 minutes. In a small saucepan, heat the stock until just boiling.

**5** Arrange the toasted bread on a warmed dish. Brush each slice of bread very lightly with just enough stock to dampen the surface. Spread the chicken liver mixture thinly on each slice of bread, then cut them in half and serve immediately.

## CROSTINI WITH MASCARPONE AND WALNUTS

### CROSTINI AL MASCARPONE E NOCI

**TIME 10 MINUTES • MAKES 24**

5 tablespoons mascarpone cheese
20 shelled walnuts, finely chopped
3 tablespoons freshly grated Parmesan
a pinch of ground cinnamon
salt and freshly milled black pepper
12 thin slices ciabatta bread or diagonal slices from a baguette, lightly toasted

**1** Mix the mascarpone with the walnuts, the Parmesan and the cinnamon.

**2** Season to taste, then spread on to the toasted bread. Cut each slice in half and serve immediately.

## PARMESAN WITH PEARS AND WALNUTS

### PARMIGIANO CON LE PERE E LE NOCI

*I can never decide which is more delicious, the flavour of Parmesan with pears or the combination of Parmesan with walnuts, so I have decided to put all these wonderful tastes together. Serve this light starter before a robust main course or to end a light summer meal.*

**TIME 15 MINUTES**

120 g/4½ oz fresh Parmesan cheese, roughly cut into wedge shapes
4 small juicy pears, peeled and quartered
8 shelled walnuts, halved

**1** Arrange the cheese in the centre of a serving dish.

**2** Place the pears around the cheese and then scatter the walnuts here and there. This dish is perfect with a rounded, full-flavoured red wine such as a Sangiovese.

## PEPPERS AND SUN-DRIED TOMATOES WITH GRILLED MOZZARELLA

### PEPERONI E POMODORI SECCHI CON MOZZARELLA

*This is a very gooey sort of dish, best if eaten with a knife and fork, sitting at the table. It is essential to serve it with bread. Although it is very good with mozzarella, it is even better when made with the sack-shaped matured mozzarella called scamorza.*

**TIME 10 MINUTES**

250 g/8 oz mozzarella, sliced
6 sun-dried tomatoes in oil, drained with oil reserved, sliced thinly
6 peppers preserved in oil, drained with oil reserved, sliced thinly
salt and freshly milled black pepper
fresh basil leaves, to garnish

**1** Heat the grill to medium.

**2** Arrange the cheese on a flame-proof serving dish. Put it under the grill for about 4 minutes, until the cheese begins to run and bubble.

**3** Remove the dish and arrange the tomatoes and peppers on top of the cheese. Pour over the reserved oils and then season with salt and pepper.

**4** Garnish with the fresh basil leaves and serve immediately with plenty of fresh bread.

**OVERLEAF**
**Left** *Peppers and sun-dried tomatoes with grilled mozzarella*
**Right** *Parmesan with pears and walnuts*

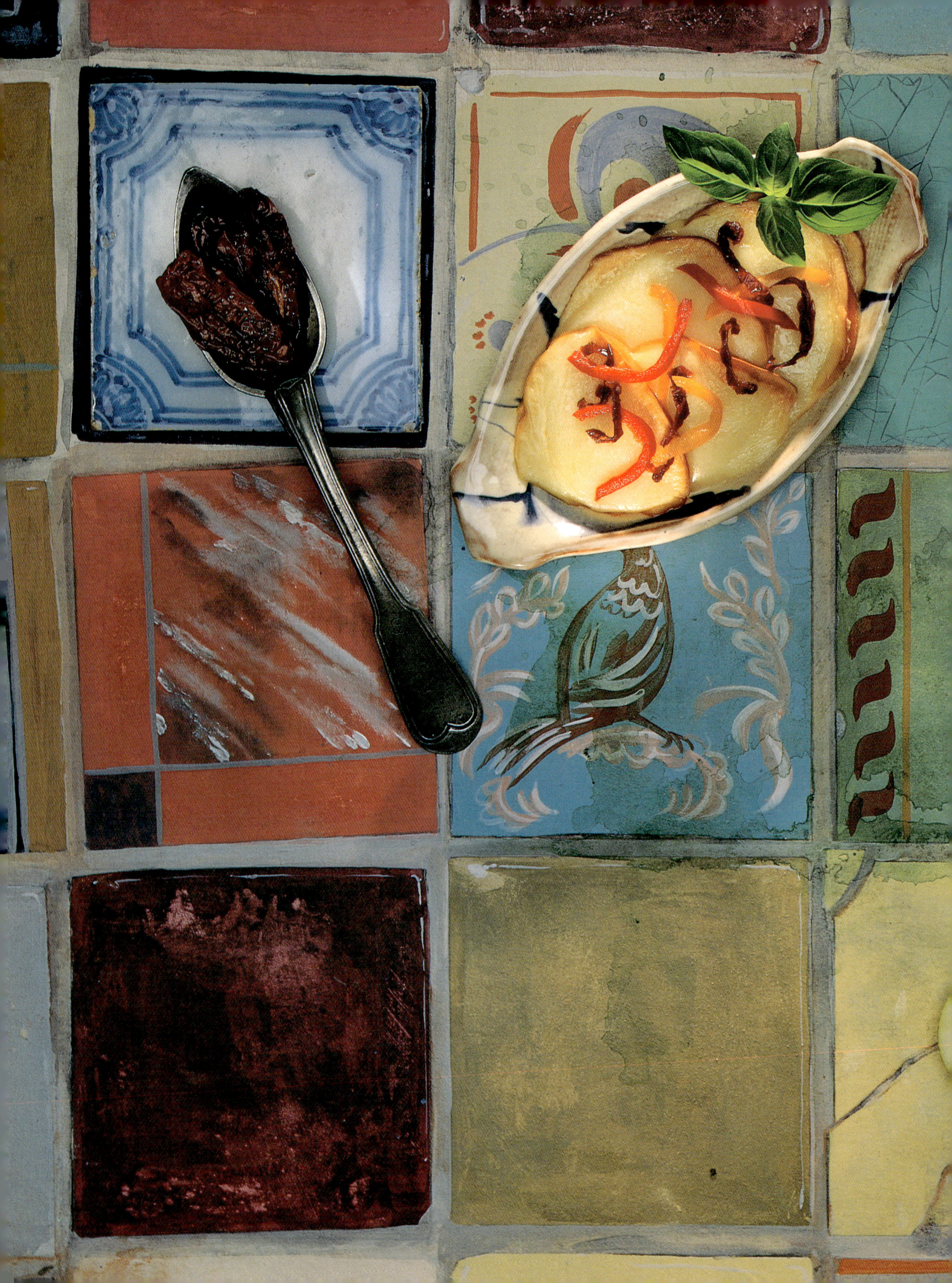

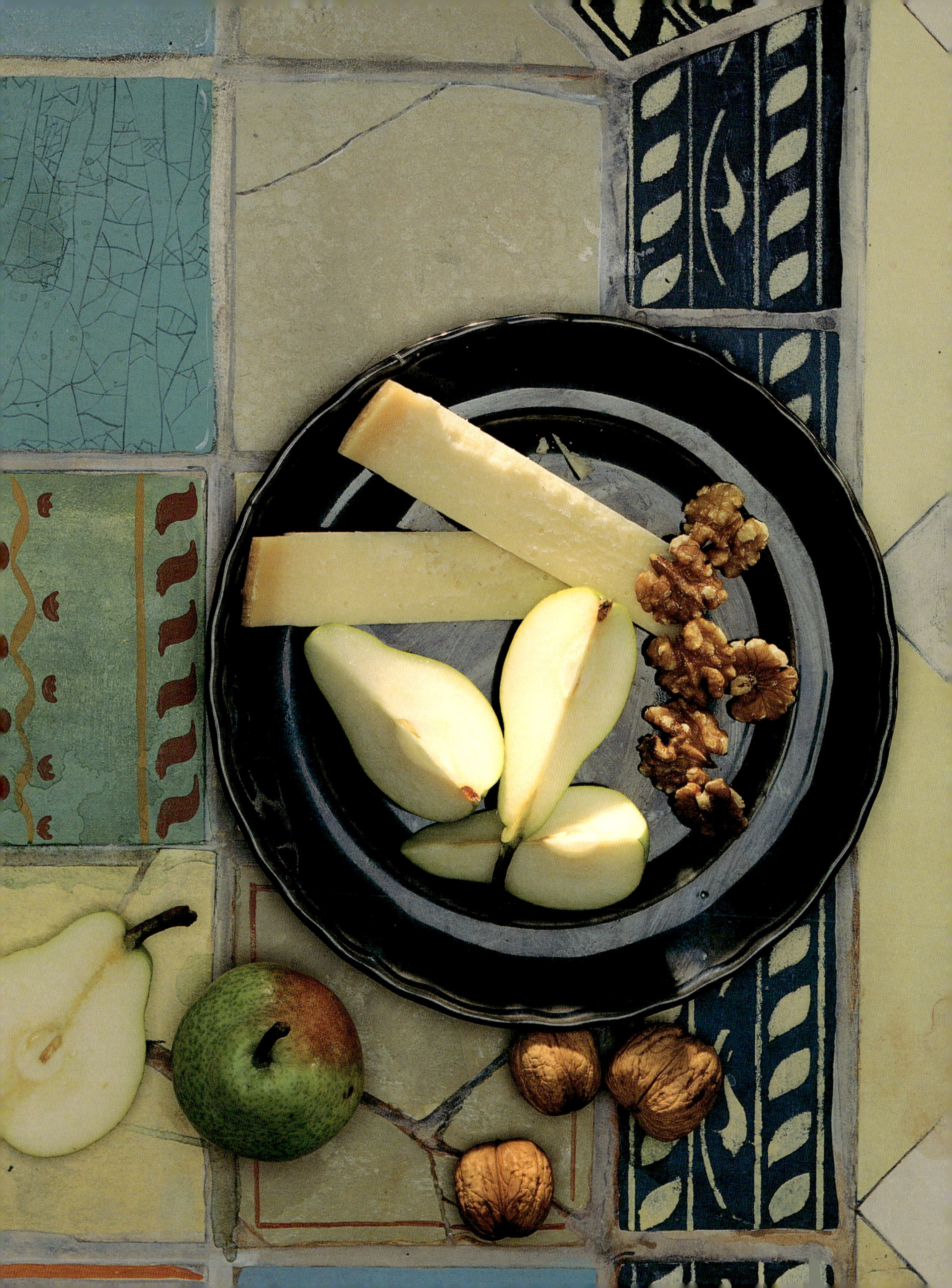

## GORGONZOLA AND PÂTÉ WITH WALNUT BREAD

### CREMA DI GORGONZOLA AL PÂTÉ CON IL PANE DE NOCI

*Use any lean meat or vegetarian pâté available at supermarkets or delicatessens. I like to use a simple or uncomplicated pork or chicken liver pâté for this recipe. If you cannot get hold of walnut bread, use thinly sliced malted brown bread instead.*

**TIME 10 MINUTES**

**100 g/4 oz lean pâté of your choice
100 g/4 oz Gorgonzola cheese
1 large onion, finely grated
savoury walnut bread (or crusty wholemeal), thinly sliced, to serve**

**1** Mash the pâté with a fork until smooth.

**2** Mash the Gorgonzola, then add to the pâté. Mix together thoroughly.

**3** Put the onions in a sieve set over a bowl and press with the back of a wooden spoon to extract all the juices. Discard the onions. Add the juices to the Gorgonzola and pâté mixture and mix together thoroughly.

**4** Serve spread thickly on to thinly sliced savoury walnut bread.

## GREEN OLIVE AND WALNUT DIP

### CREMA DI OLIVE E NOCI

*Choose a selection of interestingly flavoured grissini (breadsticks) or biscuits to dip into this marvellously crunchy dip. Supermarkets and delicatessens now stock the mass-produced thin breadsticks which have long since been a staple of Italian restaurants. These are fine, but if you are lucky enough to find the more irregular shaped home-made ones, with a variety of flavourings, do not pass them up.*

**TIME 5 MINUTES**

**250 g/8 oz green olives, stoned
100 g/4 oz walnuts, shelled
2 tablespoons freshly grated Parmesan cheese
1 tablespoon olive oil
salt and freshly milled black pepper**

**1** Put the olives and the walnuts into the food processor and whizz on full power for 30 seconds.

**2** Gradually add the grated cheese and oil with the machine still running to make a mixture which is well amalgamated but still gritty. Season with salt and pepper and serve with pre-dinner drinks.

*Green olive and walnut dip*

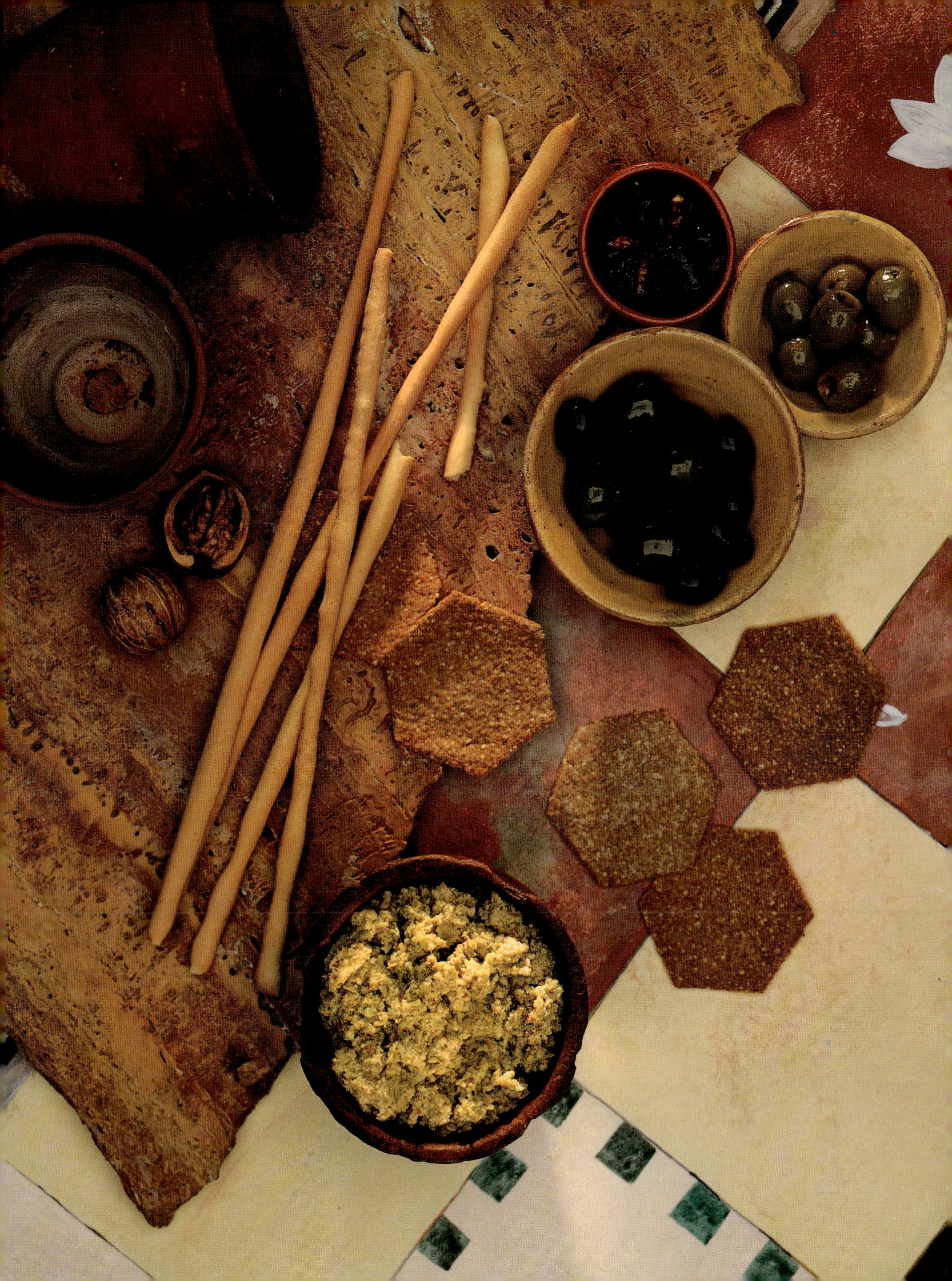

## PROSCIUTTO AND BALSAMIC VINEGAR ROLLS

### PROSCIUTTO CON ACETO BALSAMICO

*I was taught to make this dish in Modena, the home of balsamic vinegar. Focaccia, a flat bread, is an example of the wider variety of Italian breads now available in larger supermarkets. If you can't find focaccia, substitute any country-style loaf.*

**TIME 5 MINUTES**

12 thin slices prosciutto crudo
1 tablespoon balsamic vinegar
freshly milled black pepper
focaccia bread, warmed
rocket leaves, to garnish

**1** Arrange the prosciutto on a wooden board, with each slice slightly overlapping the next to make a single sheet.

**2** Sprinkle all the prosciutto lightly with the vinegar, then roll up like a swiss roll. Sprinkle generously with freshly milled black pepper.

**3** Cut the roll into 5 cm/2 in slices. Arrange the slices on a dish. Garnish with the rocket and serve at once with warmed focaccia bread.

## SALAME AND FIG BITES

### BOCCINI DI FICHI E SALAME

*If you have never tasted the exciting combination of fresh figs and salame, this is your chance! It is a typically Italian and superb marriage of tastes. Finocchiona is a very big Tuscan salame flavoured with fennel seeds. A more readily available substitute is Milano, stocked by most Italian delicatessens and large supermarkets.*

**TIME 5 MINUTES • MAKES 6**

4 large fresh black figs, peeled and quartered
16 thin slices Milano or Finocchiona salame

**1** Wrap each fig quarter in a slice of salame.

**2** Use a wooden cocktail stick to secure each closed and serve immediately, or refrigerate.

## GRILLED TOMATOES WITH CAPERS AND MARJORAM

### POMODORI ALLA GRIGLIA CON CAPPERI E MAGGIORANA

*This is a very light and simple dish that can be served as an accompanying vegetable or as an antipasto. Serve with crusty bread.*

**TIME 20 MINUTES**

4 tablespoons olive oil
5 tablespoons very fresh white breadcrumbs
50 g/2 oz salted or pickled capers, rinsed, dried and finely chopped
2 tablespoons fresh marjoram leaves or 2 teaspoons dried marjoram
8 small firm, ripe tomatoes, halved
salt and freshly milled black pepper.

**1** Heat the grill to medium. Mix half the olive oil with the breadcrumbs.

**2** Mix the capers into the oil and bread mixture. Add the marjoram and season to taste.

**3** Coat each tomato half with the mixture and pour over the remaining oil.

**4** Grill for 5 to 10 minutes until the tomatoes are heated through and are a golden crusty brown on top. Serve immediately.

## GRILLED CAPRINO IN VINE LEAVES
### CAPRINO ALLA GRIGLIA NELLE FOGLIE DI VITE

*I can never eat caprino, a tube-shaped goats' cheese often preserved in olive oil, without it reminding me of my youngest brother. Caprino cheese and fresh apricots were his favourite foods, often eaten together, and my mother would always make sure the fridge was well stocked with both whenever he was due home from boarding school in England. I guess it made him feel he had really come home to Italy again. If you cannot get hold of caprino, any soft white goats' milk or ewes' milk cheese will work equally well.*

**TIME 15 MINUTES**

**4 fresh caprino cheeses, cut in half lengthways**
**16 fresh or preserved plain vine leaves, well rinsed and dried**
**salt and freshly milled black pepper**
**olive oil**
**chopped fresh rosemary**

**1** Unwrap the cheeses if they come in a thin paper covering and put them on a board to drain a little. Heat the grill to medium.

**2** Lay each cheese half on 2 slightly overlapping vine leaves. Season with salt and pepper, a little olive oil and a sprinkling of fresh rosemary.

**3** Wrap the 2 leaves tightly around each piece of cheese and secure with wooden cocktail sticks.

**4** Grill the cheese parcels for about 2 minutes on each side until the leaves are just browned and the cheese is soft but not runny. Arrange on a warmed platter, remove the cocktail sticks and serve immediately.

## DEEP-FRIED SAGE LEAVES
### SALVIA FRITTA

*This is an unusual teaser to serve with a glass of sparkling wine before a meal. The flavour of fresh sage is much less intense than dried sage, but nevertheless the overall taste is quite pungent. Most importantly, the fried sage clusters must be served as hot as possible.*

**TIME 15 MINUTES**

**8 small tufts of fresh sage leaves, as young and tender as possible, rinsed and patted dry**
**2 eggs, separated**
**2 tablespoons self-raising flour**
**salt**
**oil for deep-frying**

**1** Pick over the sage with care, making sure that each leaf is perfectly dry.

**2** Beat the egg yolks until pale and light, then sift in the flour and blend to make a light batter. Whisk the egg whites until stiff, then fold them into the batter.

**3** Heat the oil until a small piece of bread dropped into the oil sizzles instantly.

**4** Dip the sage into the batter to coat it completely, then fry for about 1 minute until golden brown and crisp all over. Drain the leaves thoroughly on kitchen paper and sprinkle with salt. Serve at once.

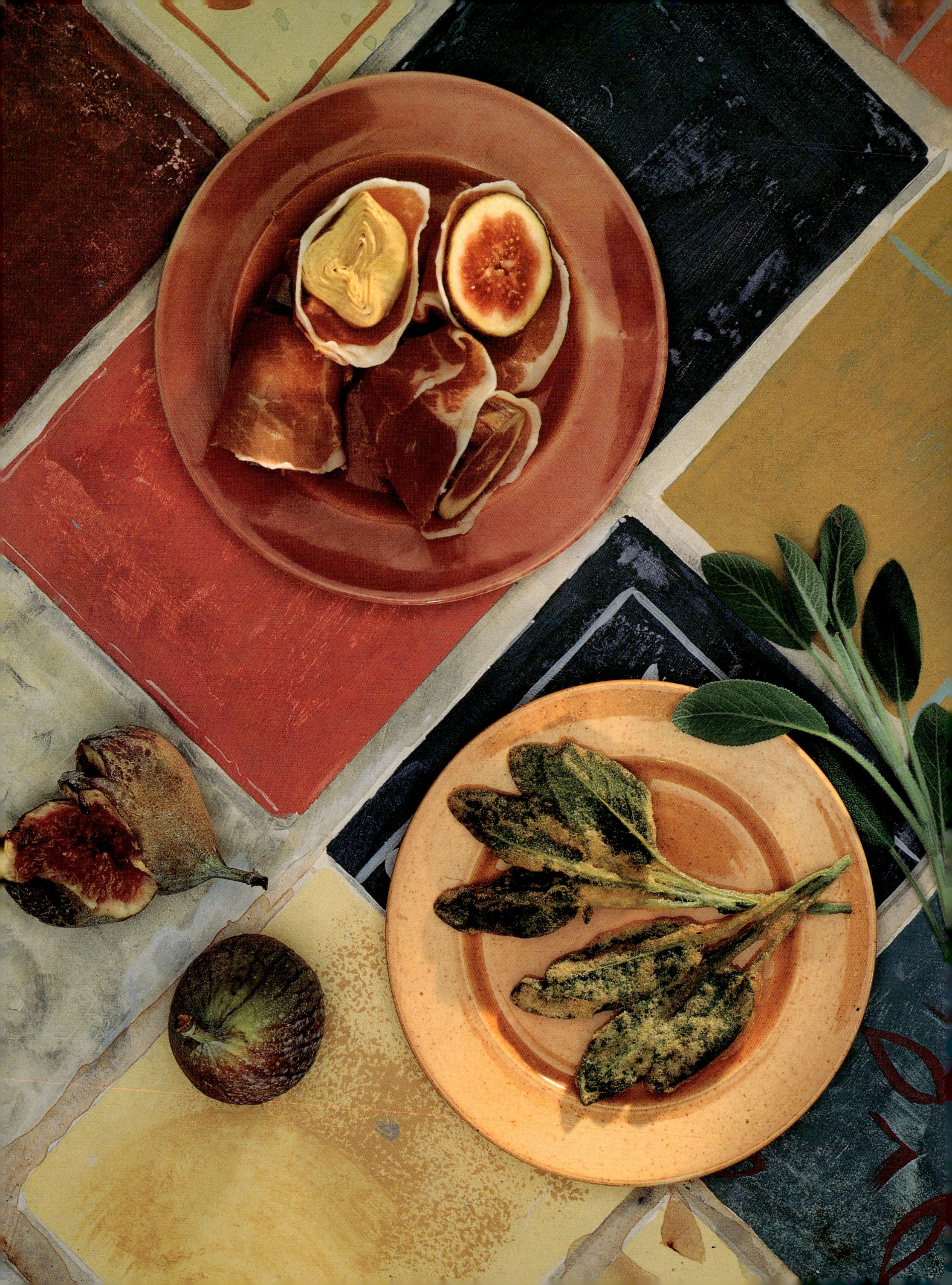

ANTIPASTI AND STARTERS 31

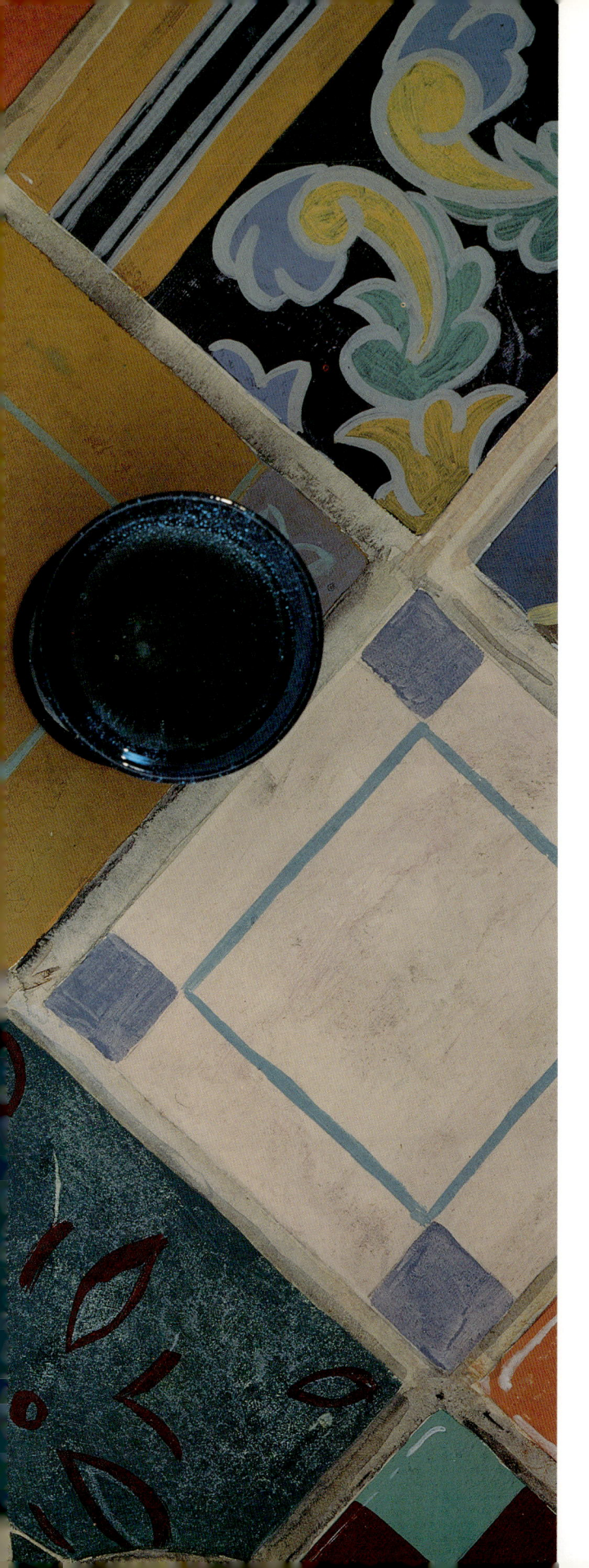

## PROSCIUTTO PARCELS

### PACCHETTINI DI PROSCIUTTO

*For a very light start to the meal you will only need one parcel each, yet if you want more, simply increase the quantities accordingly.*

**TIME 5 MINUTES**

**4 very thin slices prosciutto crudo
4 marinated artichoke hearts or
 4 fresh black figs, peeled**

**1** Lay the slices of prosciutto side by side on a chopping board.

**2** Place the artichoke hearts or figs at one end of each slice. Roll up the slice of prosciutto to encase the artichoke heart or fig completely.

**3** Fold in the edges and secure with a wooden cocktail stick.

**4** Serve immediately, or refrigerate.

**Above** *Prosciutto parcels*
**Below** *Deep-fried sage leaves*

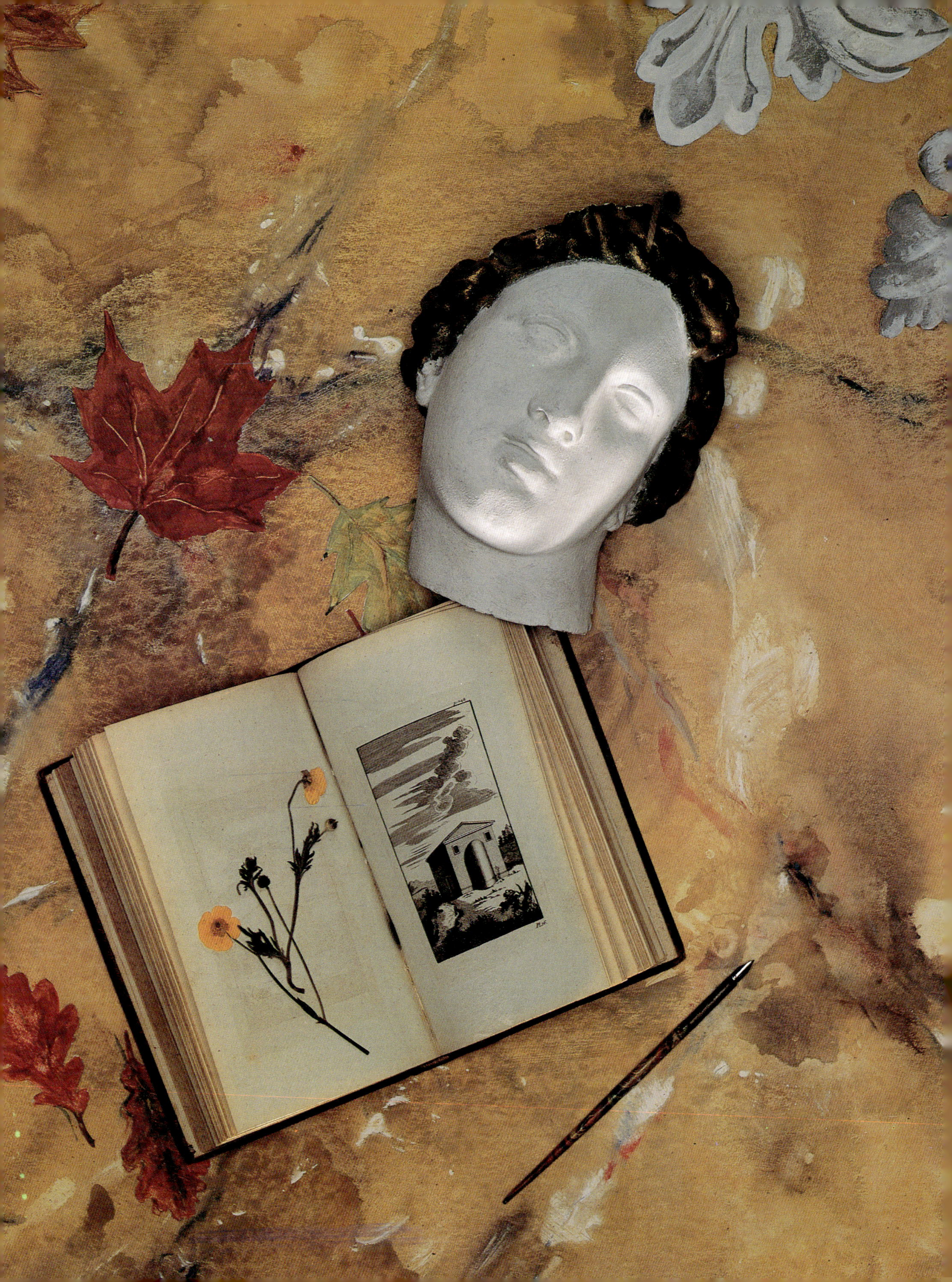

# LIGHT SNACKS

*We all love being able to throw together original snacks with minimum effort. Italian ingredients are superb for using as a topping on toasted bread or serving with a selection of fruit.*

## BRUSCHETTA WITH TOMATOES AND RED ONIONS

### BRUSCHETTA CON POMODORO E CIPOLLE ROSSE

*Originally, bruschetta was simply slices of bread, lightly rubbed with garlic, sprinkled with olive oil and then dusted with salt and pepper. Yet from these humble beginnings, bruschetta has evolved to include a variety of toppings so that it is now more of a warm open sandwich than merely a version of garlic bread.*

TIME (USING CANNED TOMATOES) 15 MINUTES; (USING FRESH TOMATOES) 25 MINUTES

- 1 large red onion, peeled and coarsely chopped
- 5 tablespoons olive oil
- 10 canned or very ripe fresh tomatoes
- salt and freshly milled black pepper
- 4 large slices ciabatta bread or other coarse Italian bread
- 1 garlic clove, peeled
- chopped fresh parsley, to garnish
- 8 thin slices red onion, to garnish

**1** Gently fry the onion in a frying pan with three-quarters of the oil for about 10 minutes, until soft, stirring frequently.

**2** Meanwhile, prepare the tomatoes. If you are using canned tomatoes, they simply need to be drained and coarsely chopped. If you are using fresh tomatoes, they need to be blanched in boiling water for about 1 minute, then peeled, seeded and coarsely chopped.

**3** Add the tomatoes to the onions, season with salt and pepper and heat through while you prepare the bread.

**4** Heat the grill and toast the bread lightly on both sides. Rub lightly on both sides with the garlic.

**5** Arrange the bread slices on a platter and sprinkle with the remaining oil. Spoon the hot tomato and onion mixture over each slice of bread. Sprinkle with parsley and lay 2 slices of raw onion on top of each bruschetta. Serve at once. You can, of course, cut the bread into smaller pieces and make crostini-sized servings, if you prefer.

## TOMATO AND OLIVE CROSTINI WITH CAPERS

### CROSTINI CON POMODORO E OLIVE E CAPPERI

*The idea of crostini is to savour them whilst drinking a pre-prandial glass of wine. Although they are sometimes served at the table, it is most usual to eat them as finger food before the meal so do not overload them or the sauce will fall off! These are also perfect as little snacks served on their own.*

TIME (USING CANNED TOMATOES) 15 MINUTES; (USING FRESH TOMATOES) 25 MINUTES

- 1 medium-sized white French baguette, cut into thumb-thick slices
- 5 tablespoons olive oil
- 10 canned or very ripe fresh tomatoes
- 12 stoned black olives, coarsely chopped
- 1½ tablespoons salted capers, rinsed and dried
- salt and freshly milled black pepper
- 2 garlic cloves, peeled

**1** Arrange the slices of bread in the grill pan in an even layer.

**2** Put 3 tablespoons of the oil into a large frying pan. If you are using canned tomatoes they will simply need to be drained then coarsely chopped. If you are using fresh tomatoes, they will need to be blanched in boiling water for about 1 minute, then peeled, seeded and chopped.

**3** Add the tomatoes to the oil and cook together very quickly for about 10 minutes, stirring constantly, then add the olives and capers. Season with salt and pepper.

**4** Heat the grill and toast the bread lightly on both sides. Rub the hot toast with the garlic very generously and then arrange on a serving platter. Sprinkle with the remaining oil. Spoon a little of the tomato, olive and caper mixture on top of each slice of toast and serve at once.

**Above** *Tomato and olive crostini with capers*
**Below** *Bruschetta with tomatoes and red onions*

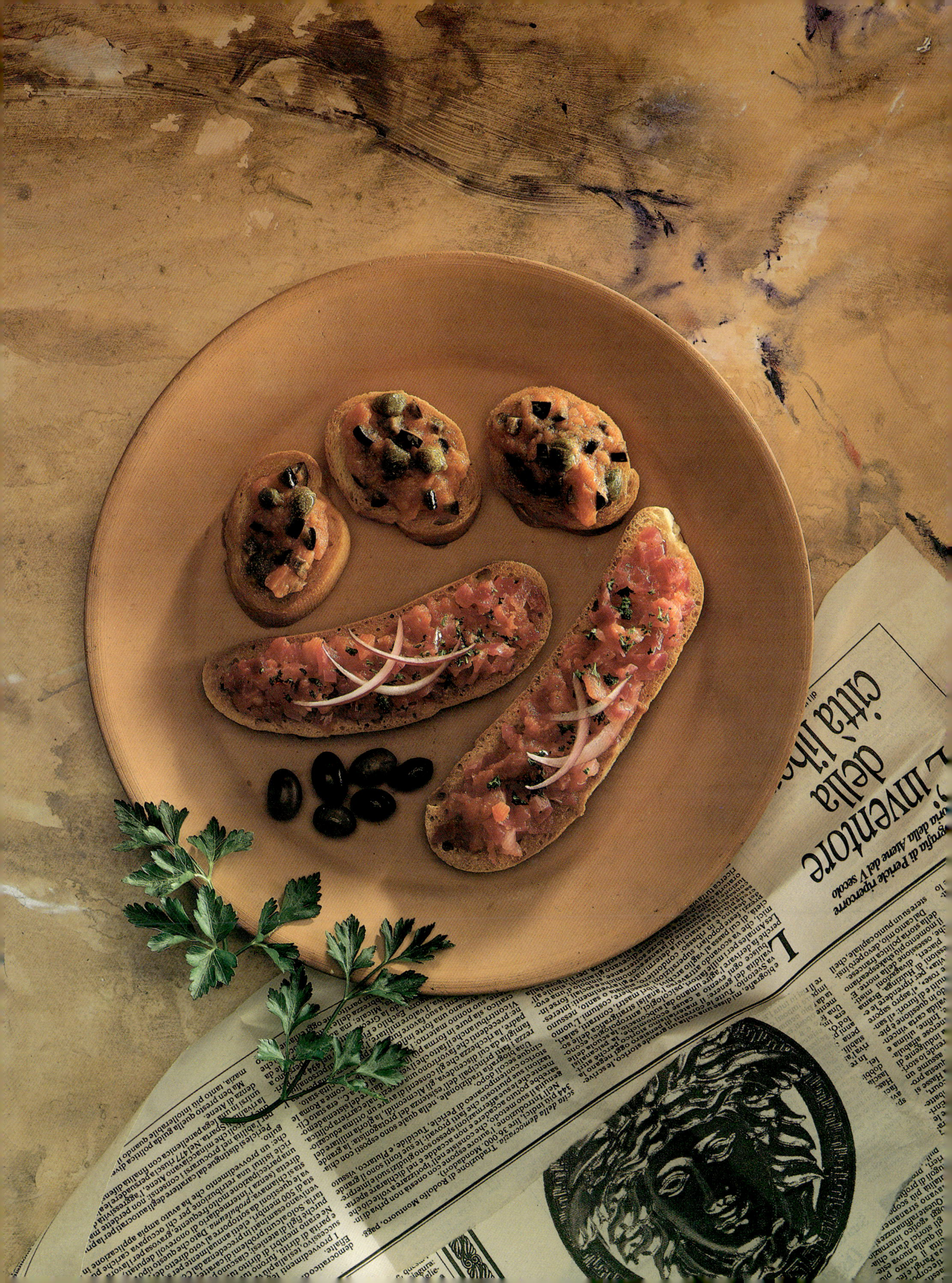

## BLACK OLIVE, LEMON AND LEEK SALAD

### INSALATA DI OLIVE NERE, LIMONI E PORRI

*This is a very strong-flavoured salad, ideal for waking up tired taste buds! It is a bit unusual to eat lemon rind, but it does actually blend very well with the other intense flavours.*

**TIME 20 MINUTES • SERVES 4-6**

400 g/14 oz black olives, stoned
4 medium-sized leeks, washed
  and very thinly sliced
2 thin-skinned unwaxed lemons,
  washed and dried
4 tablespoons olive oil
salt and freshly milled black pepper
2 tablespoons chopped fresh parsley
crusty bread, to serve

**1** Mix the olives together in a bowl with the leeks.

**2** Top and tail the lemons and discard the end sections. Slice the lemons very finely, then quarter all the slices. Remove any pips. Add the lemon segments, skin included, to the salad.

**3** Stir in enough olive oil to make everything shiny. Season with salt and pepper to taste, then mix in the parsley. Leave to stand for about 10 minutes to allow the oil to soak into the lemons. Serve with plenty of bread for soaking up the oil.

## BROAD BEAN AND PECORINO SALAD

### INSALATA DI FAVE E PECORINO

*The combination of the beans and strongly flavoured ewes' milk cheese is fantastic, especially with the oil that marries the tastes together. Serve with bread for soaking up the extra oil.*

**TIME 5 MINUTES**

1.5 kg/3 lb fresh broad beans, with pods
salt and freshly milled black pepper
250 g/8 oz pecorino cheese, cut into small pieces
3 tablespoons olive oil

**1** Shell the beans and skin if the beans are very large.

**2** Blanch the beans for 1 minute in boiling salted water. Drain well and transfer to a salad bowl.

**3** Add the cheese and oil. Then mix together and season with plenty of salt and black pepper.

**4** Arrange in a serving bowl and serve at once.

## BORLOTTI BEAN AND PRAWN SALAD
### INSALATA DI GAMBERETTI E BORLOTTI

**TIME 20 MINUTES**

250 g/8 oz can borlotti beans, drained and rinsed
250 g/8 oz peeled prawns (defrost if frozen)
juice of ½ lemon
salt and freshly milled black pepper
4-6 tablespoons olive oil
1-2 teaspoons chopped fresh coriander or chervil, to garnish

**1** Mix the beans together with the prawns in a bowl.

**2** Mix the lemon juice with a big pinch of salt and about ½ teaspoon pepper.

**3** Stir in the oil (about 4 tablespoons but use more or less according to taste) and then pour over the beans and prawns. Mix together carefully, garnish with the coriander or chervil and leave to stand for at least 10 minutes before serving.

**4** Give the salad a quick stir before serving.

## BUTTER BEAN AND MOCK CAVIAR SALAD
### INSALATA DI FAGIOLONI BIANCHI E CAVIALE FINTO

*There is, of course, nothing to stop you using real caviar from a sturgeon if you feel that way inclined, or as a compromise you could choose some salmon caviar, which is really very good and not all that expensive. Nothing is quicker than this instant salad or starter. Don't leave the salad to stand because the caviar will seep and the whole thing will take on a revolting grey appearance.*

**TIME 2 MINUTES**

300 g/11 oz can butter beans, drained
1-2  50 g/2 oz jars mock caviar (black lumpfish roe)
5 tablespoons olive oil
1-2 heaped tablespoons finely chopped onion
salt and freshly milled black pepper
chopped fresh parsley, to garnish

Mix all the ingredients together thoroughly and serve immediately. Just toss everything together, check the seasoning and adjust if necessary, and serve, garnished with a little chopped parsley.

**OVERLEAF**
Left *Broad bean and pecorino salad* and *borlotti bean and prawn salad*
Right *Butter bean and mock caviar salad*

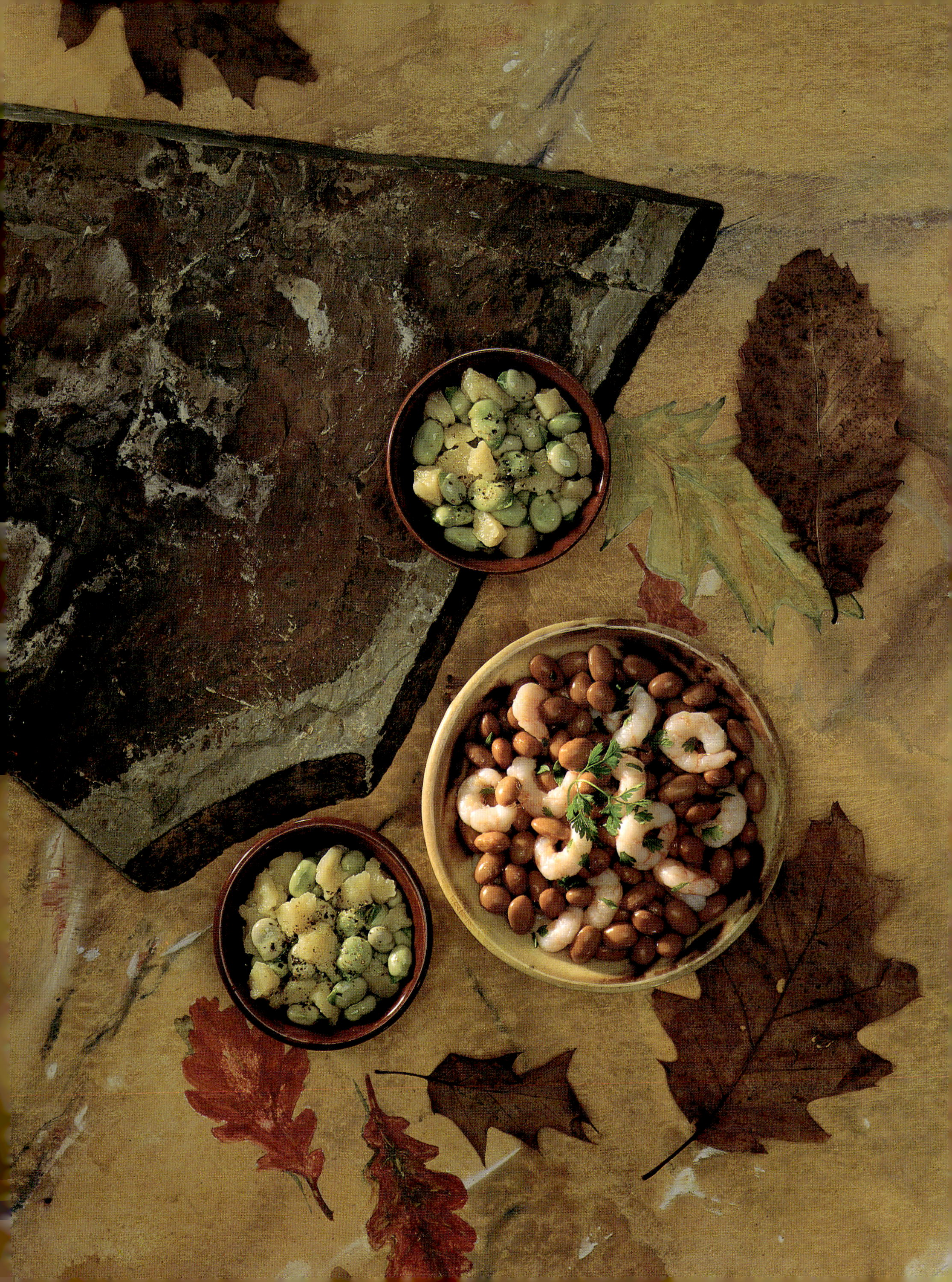

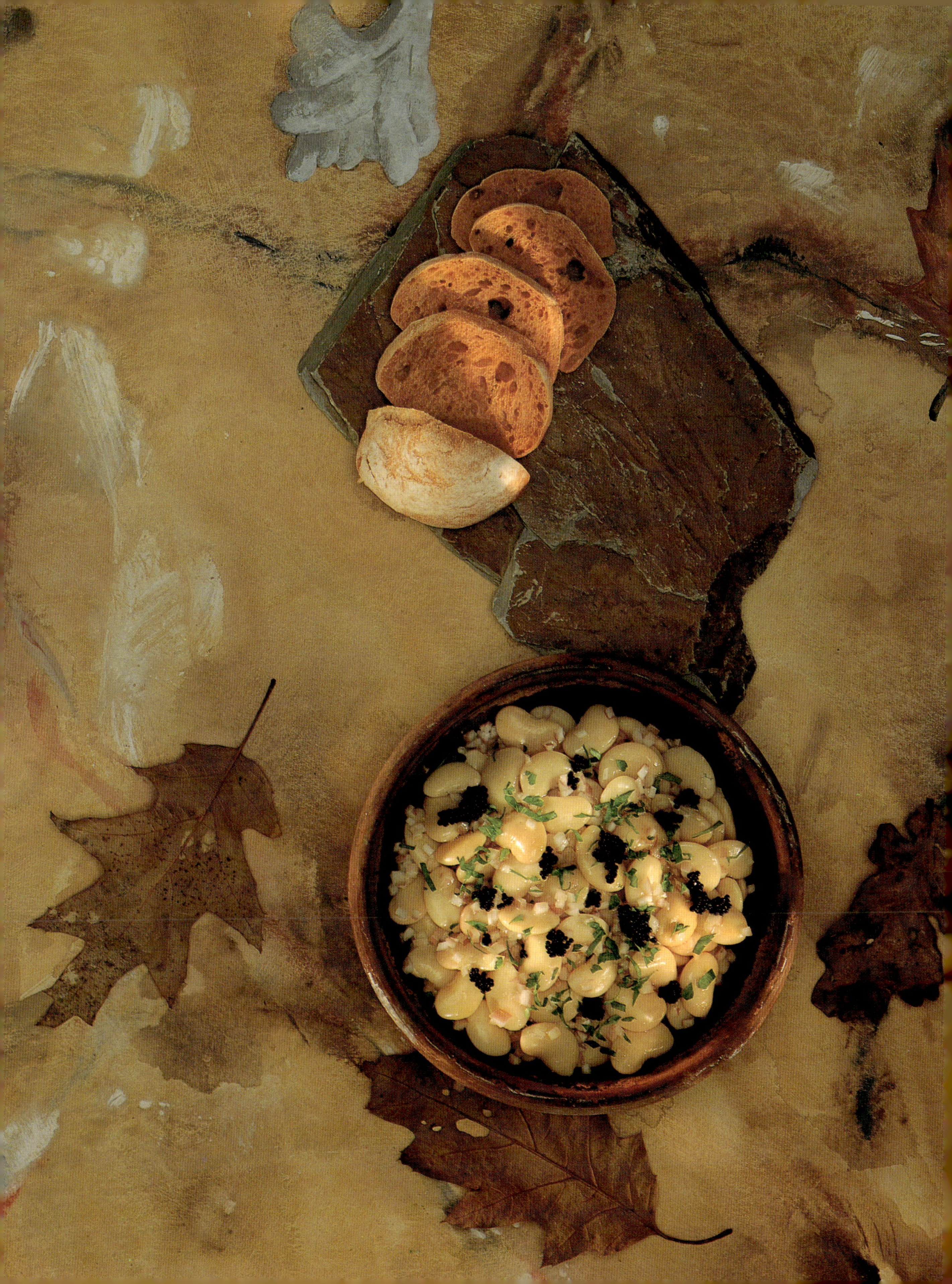

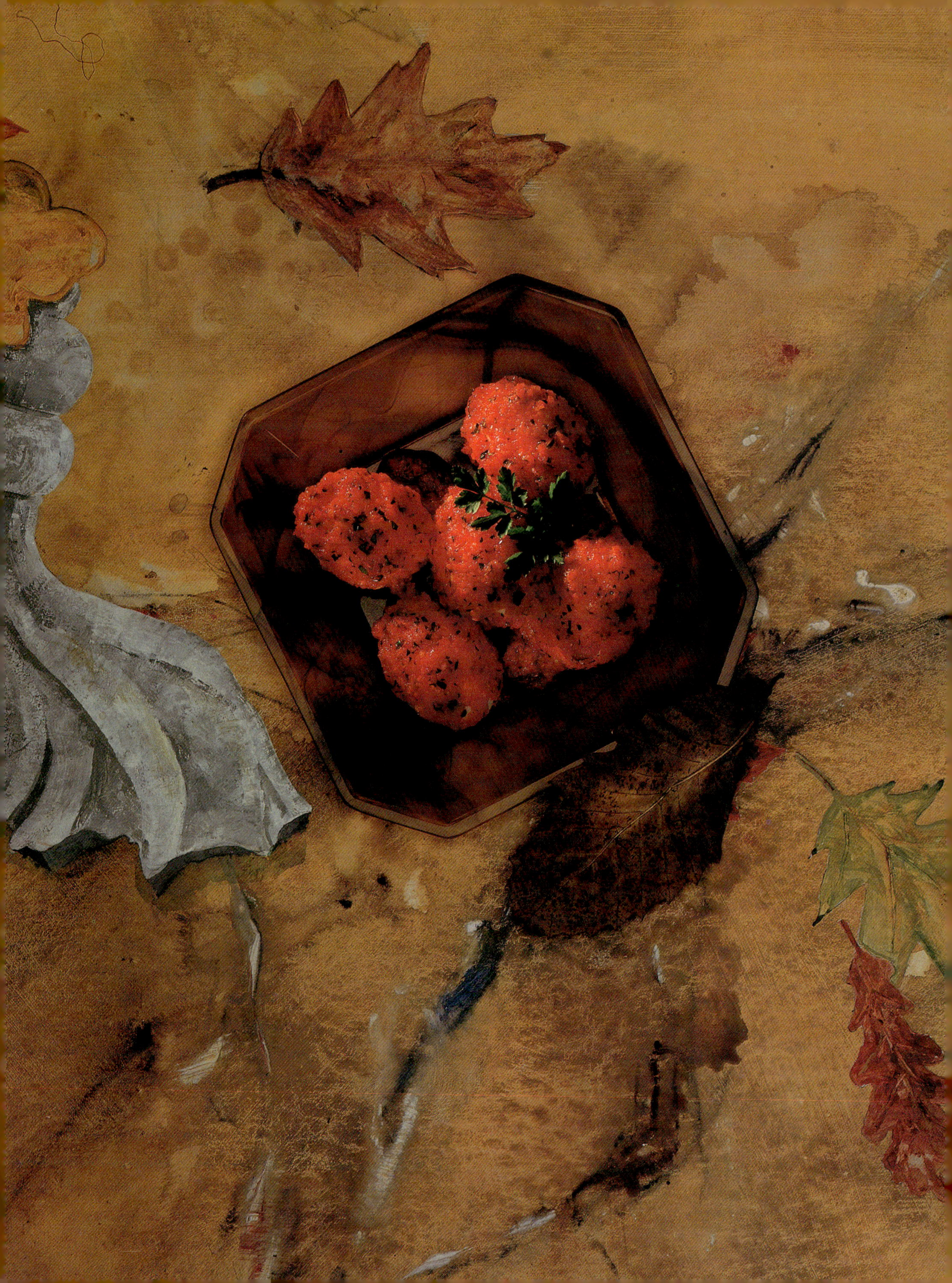

## EGGS IN A RED PEPPER SAUCE

**UOVA CON SALSA DI PEPERONI ROSSI**

*This is an interesting and very pretty alternative to an ordinary egg mayonnaise.*

**TIME 20 MINUTES**

2 large red peppers, thinly sliced
2 onions, chopped
1 handful of fresh parsley, chopped
3 tablespoons olive oil
4 canned tomatoes, sieved
salt and freshly milled black pepper
4 eggs, hard-boiled, shelled and halved

**1** Put the peppers and onions in a food processor and reduce to a fine mass. Add the parsley and whizz again then transfer the mixture to a saucepan with the oil.

**2** Bring to the boil and boil quickly to reduce by about half. Remove from the heat and stir in the tomatoes. Season generously with salt and pepper and set aside.

**3** Arrange the eggs yolkside down on a serving dish. Spoon the sauce all over the eggs, then serve at once or refrigerate.

*Eggs in a red pepper sauce*

## PLUM TOMATOES STUFFED WITH TUNA AND OLIVES

**POMODORINI A PERA RIPIENI DI TONNO E OLIVE**

*I don't know whether it is just the shape of plum tomatoes that makes them seem like they taste different, or whether they really do taste different to round tomatoes! Either way, the filling is perfect for both shapes, but I like plum tomatoes best because they remind me more of Italy!*

**TIME 15 MINUTES**

**8 fresh plum tomatoes, halved lengthways
400 g/14 oz canned tuna in brine, well drained
12 black olives, stoned and chopped
3 tablespoons mayonnaise
salt and freshly milled black pepper
fresh basil leaves to garnish
salted capers, rinsed and dried, to garnish**

**1** Scoop out the seeds and membranes from inside the tomatoes and sieve to extract the juice.

**2** Flake the tuna and mix it with the tomato juice, olives and mayonnaise. Season with salt and pepper and mix together.

**3** Spoon this mixture into the halved tomatoes, piling it as high as you like.

**4** Garnish with the fresh basil and a few capers and serve at once.

## MOZZARELLA SALAD WITH CAPERS AND OLIVES

**INSALATA DI MOZZARELLA CON CAPPERI E OLIVE**

*I like the tangy, sour taste of the capers and olives with the fresh blandness of the cheese. If you cannot get hold of the* cigliegine, *which are mozzarella balls, use a large mozzarella, neatly cubed.*

**TIME 5 MINUTES**

**24 small mozzarella balls, *cigliegine*, or
    300 g/11 oz (dry weight) mozzarella, cubed
2 tablespoons salted capers, rinsed and dried
20 mixed black and green olives, stoned
small handful of fresh parsley, finely chopped
2-4 tablespoons olive oil
freshly milled black pepper**

**1** Mix the mozzarella with the capers and olives. Scatter over the parsley.

**2** Pour the oil all over the salad, season with freshly milled black pepper and serve at once, arranged on a platter.

## PEPPERS WITH GARLIC AND ANCHOVIES
### PEPERONI CON AGLIO E ALICI

*Although this dish is quick to make, and tastes perfectly delicious minutes after you've made it, it does taste even better if it is left to stand for a while so that the flavours develop. The secret lies in the juiciness of the peppers.*

**TIME 15 MINUTES**

3 large, ripe, juicy peppers – any colours, rinsed and dried
3 garlic cloves, crushed
salt and freshly milled black pepper
2 teaspoons anchovy paste
olive oil
chopped fresh parsley, to garnish

**1** Heat the grill to medium.

**2** Grill the peppers, turning frequently, until the skins blacken and blister all over. This should take about 8 minutes.

**3** Remove the peppers from the grill and quickly rub them with a soft cloth to remove all the blackened skin. Remove whatever is left with a small sharp knife. You will end up with slightly soft, skinned peppers.

**4** Cut them in half and remove all the seeds and membranes. Slice them in half again and lay them flat on a plate, making sure no burnt bits are left.

**5** Mix the garlic with the salt and pepper, then stir in the anchovy paste. Thin with enough oil to make a dressing which will coat all the peppers lightly.

**6** Pour the dressing over the peppers, sprinkle with the parsley and set aside until ready to serve, for about 10 minutes. When completely cool, you can refrigerate them until required.

## PROSCIUTTO WITH MANGO AND PAPAYA
### PROSCIUTTO CON MANGO E PAPAYA

*Once upon a time, the only acceptable fruit to serve with prosciutto was melon. Italian chefs have since discovered the delights of prosciutto with the rich, lusty flavours of tropical fruits. Alternatively, try putting together some good-quality prosciutto with a really juicy pear.*

**TIME 5 MINUTES**

2 mangos, peeled, stoned and sliced
2 papayas, peeled and sliced
12 slices of prosciutto crudo

Arrange the fruit and ham alternately on a pretty serving platter. Serve at once with some deliciously fresh ciabatta bread and some light and crisp Valpollicella wine.

**OVERLEAF**
**Left** *Peppers with garlic and anchovies*
**Right** *Prosciutto with mango and papaya*

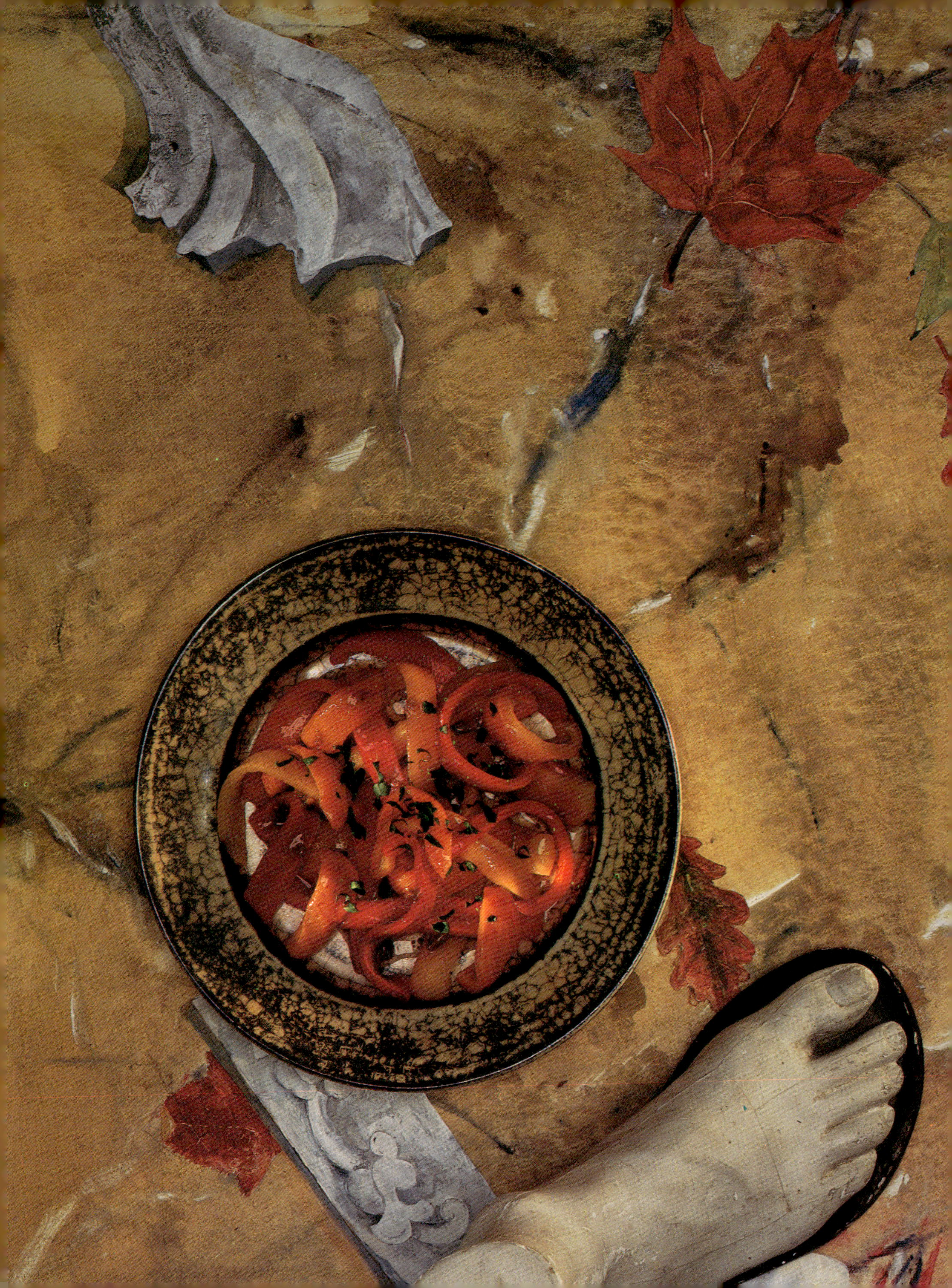

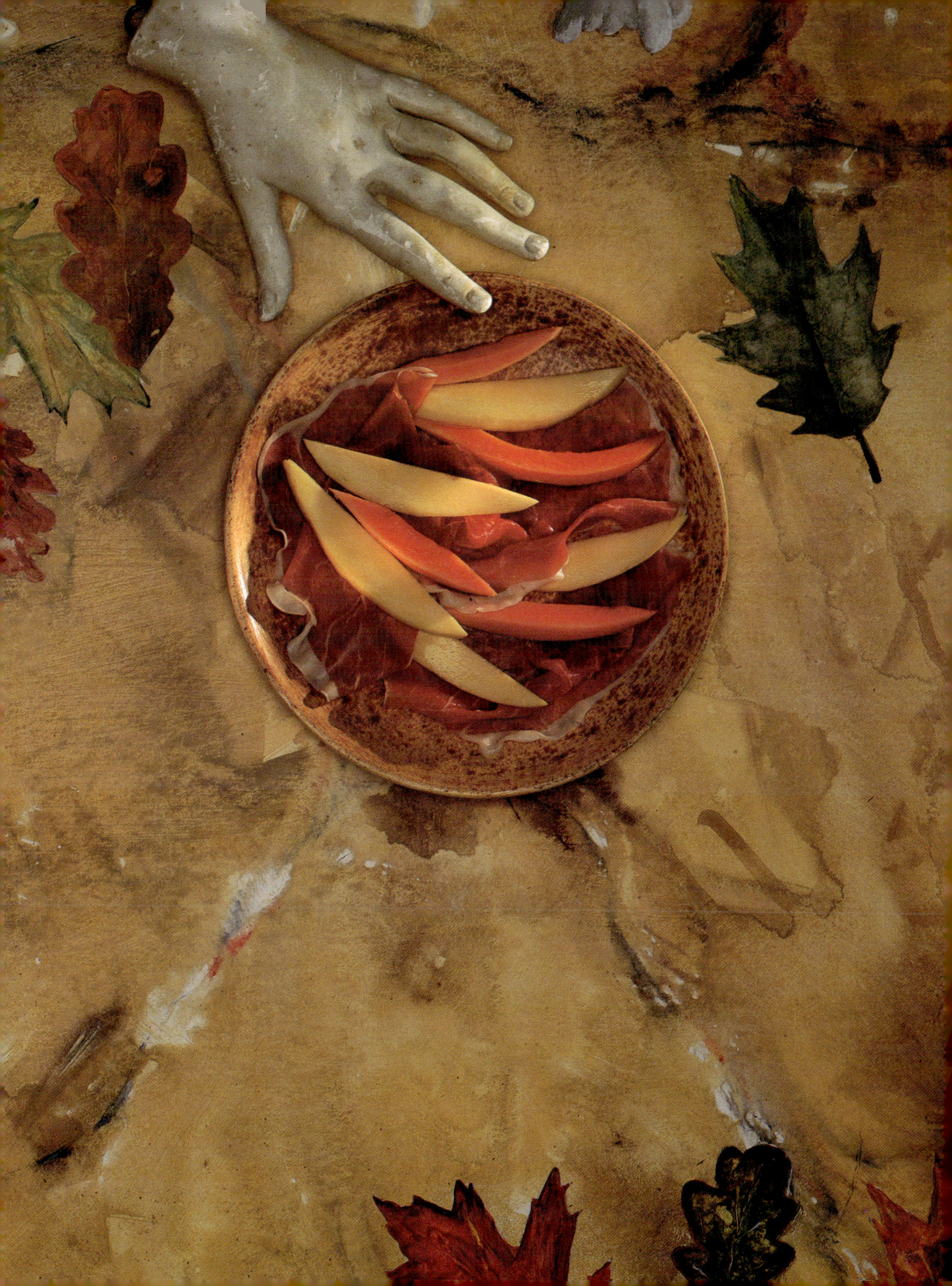

## BRUSCHETTA WITH MELTED PARMESAN CHEESE

### BRUSCHETTA CON IL PARMIGIANO

*For the cheese to achieve the right melting texture it has to be very, very fresh, preferably from a cheese which has only just been opened up and even better if slightly young. You will have to buy it in a chunk, and then slice it into ribbons using a potato peeler. I like to use a long thin loaf like a baguette (called* frusta *in Italian) and cut it open horizontally, then in half again to make sections which are about 15 cm/6 in long.*

**TIME 10 MINUTES**

**1 small baguette, sliced in sections**
**2 garlic cloves, peeled**
**5 tablespoons olive oil**
**150 g/5 oz Parmesan cheese, cut into ribbons**
**freshly milled black pepper**

**1** Heat the grill. Toast the bread lightly on the cut side only.

**2** Rub the hot toasts firmly with the garlic. Brush half the olive oil on the cut side of the toasts only.

**3** Cover each slice of toast with cheese. Return to the grill for 1-2 minutes, just until the cheese begins to melt and soften.

**4** Arrange the toasts on a warmed serving platter and brush generously with the remaining olive oil. Grind a little black pepper over the finished dish and serve.

## SUN-DRIED TOMATOES AND PROSCIUTTO ON CIABATTA

### PANE CIABATTA CON PROSCIUTTO CRUDO E POMODORI SECCHI

*These are delicious open sandwiches, perfect for* al fresco *snacking. If you prefer, you can chop the tomatoes into thin strips.*

**TIME 5 MINUTES • MAKES 8 SLICES**

**8 slices ciabatta bread, or other coarse Italian bread**
**32 sun-dried tomatoes in oil, well drained with oil reserved**
**8 slices prosciutto crudo**
**juice of ½ lemon**
**freshly milled black pepper**

**1** Warm the bread for about 3 minutes in a preheated oven at 190C/375F/Gas mark 5. Arrange the warmed slices of bread on a pretty serving platter.

**2** Drizzle the oil from the sun-dried tomatoes all over the bread.

**3** Place 2 sun-dried tomatoes on top of each slice of bread. Cover with the slices of prosciutto, folding the slices over where necessary.

**4** Place 2 sun-dried tomatoes on top of the prosciutto slices. Sprinkle each of the sandwiches with a few drops of lemon juice, then top with black pepper, and serve at once.

## MELTED SCAMORZA ON TOASTED CIABATTA

### SCAMORZA ALLA GRIGLIA SULLA CIABATTA

*This recipe is an adaptation of a dish that my family has always prepared on the barbecue for summer feasts. Scamorza, a matured and sometimes smoked mozzarella, has a wonderfully firm texture that goes soft and gooey when cooked. If you can't get scamorza, use a well-drained mozzarella that is not too fresh and soft.*

**TIME 10 MINUTES • MAKES 8**

**8 slices ciabatta bread, or other coarse Italian bread**
**2 small smoked scamorza cheeses, or 300 g/11 oz mozzarella (dry weight), sliced thinly or grated**
**5 tablespoons olive oil**
**salt and freshly milled black pepper**
**2 tablespoons very finely chopped fresh sage leaves, or 1 teaspoon very fine dried sage or ground bay leaves**

**1** Heat the grill. Toast the bread on one side only. Turn over and brush each with olive oil, then arrange all the cheese on the top.

**2** Brush generously with olive oil, season with salt and pepper and sprinkle with the sage leaves or ground bay leaves.

**3** Return to the grill and cook until the cheese is soft without being runny. Regulate the heat with care so the cheese melts without burning the bread. Serve at once, sprinkled with any remaining olive oil.

## CODDLED EGGS WITH PROSCIUTTO AND PARMESAN

### UOVA AL FORNO CON PROSCIUTTO CRUDO E PARMIGIANO

**TIME 20-25 MINUTES**

**butter for greasing ramekins**
**4 thin slices of prosciutto crudo**
**4 eggs, kept at room temperature until required**
**75 g/3 oz Parmesan cheese, freshly grated**
**8 tablespoons single cream**
**salt and freshly milled black pepper**
**2 tablespoons fresh breadcrumbs**

**1** Heat the oven to 190C/375F/Gas mark 5. Lightly butter 4 ramekins and then line each with a slice of prosciutto. Trim off excess prosciutto with scissors and use as extra lining in the ramekins.

**2** Break an egg into each ramekin. Beat the Parmesan and cream together and season with a little salt and pepper.

**3** Divide the cheese mixture between the 4 ramekins and sprinkle with the breadcrumbs.

**4** Put the ramekins in a baking tin containing enough hot water to come just halfway up the sides. Bake for 15 minutes or until the mixture is just set. Serve immediately.

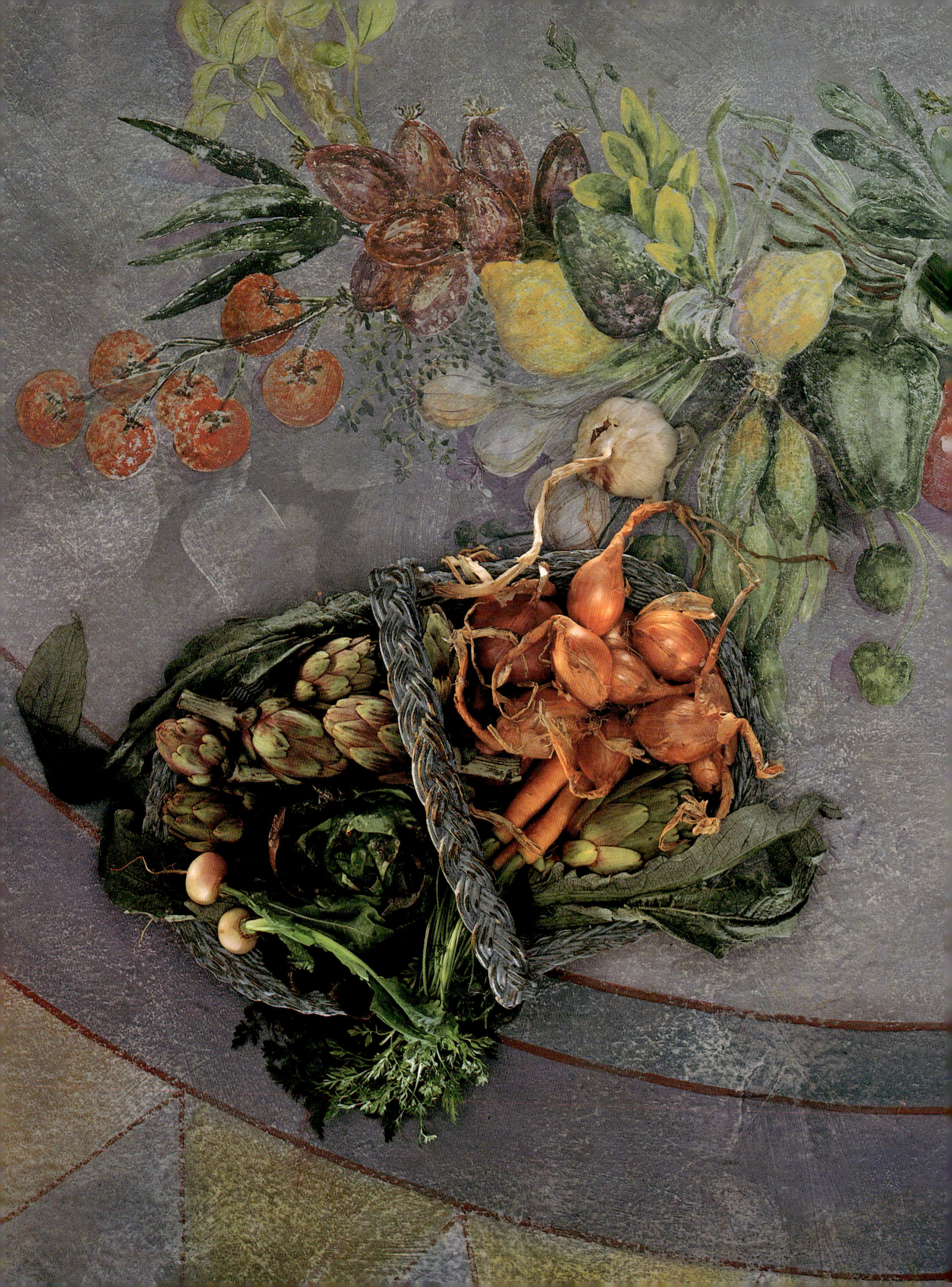

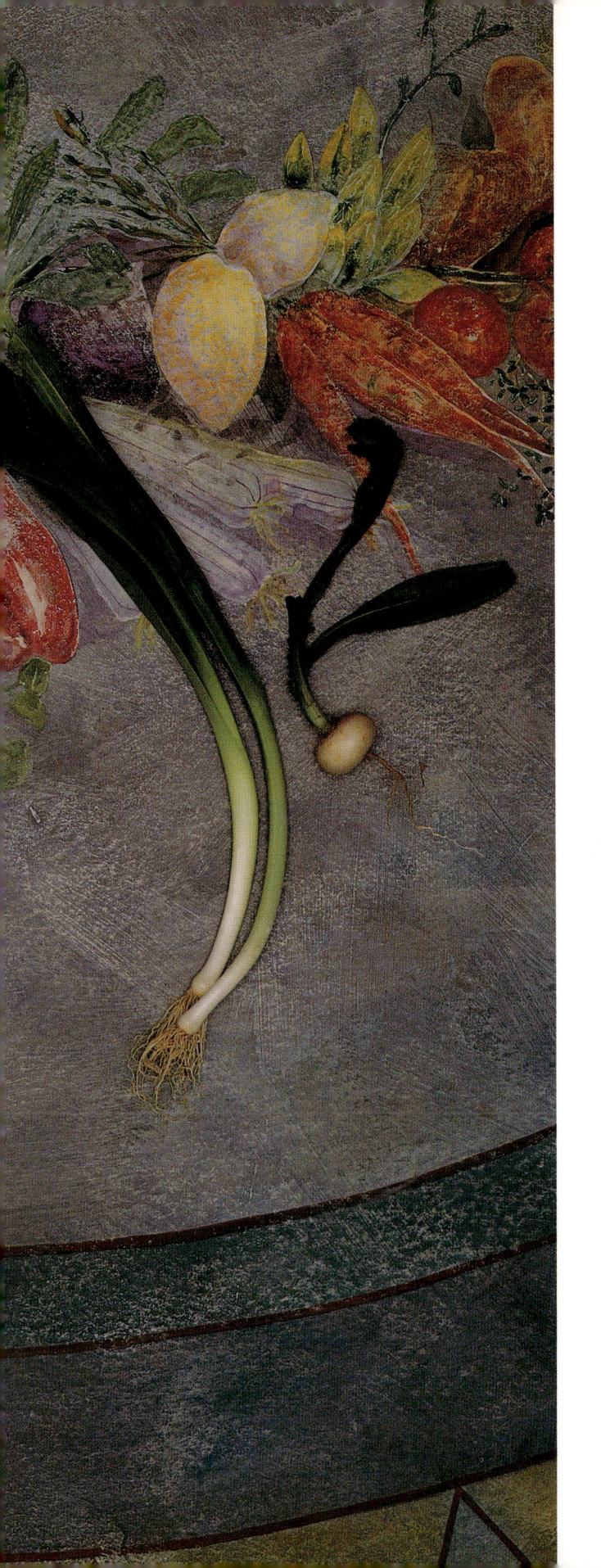

# SALADS

*Salads have become so much more interesting now that international vegetables are available virtually all year round; the salads here are as versatile and unusual as possible.*

## BREAD, TUNA AND BASIL SALAD
### INSALATA DI PANE, TONNO E BASILICO

*If you are feeling really creative, make this salad in two or more layers, doubling the quantities, structuring it so you can almost cut it into wedges to serve. Use the juiciest and firmest tomatoes and do not be afraid to press down into the bread firmly so it absorbs the liquid. Use the best quality tuna you can find as well.*

**TIME 5 MINUTES**

6 slices of ciabatta bread, or other coarse Italian bread
400 g/14 oz tuna fish in oil, well drained and flaked
4 small tomatoes, quartered
1 handful of fresh basil leaves, torn into pieces
5 tablespoons olive oil
1 tablespoon white wine vinegar
salt and freshly milled black pepper

**1** Arrange the bread in the bottom of a salad bowl.

**2** Toss the tuna, tomatoes and basil together. Sprinkle the mixture with the oil, vinegar and a little salt and pepper. Toss again.

**3** Carefully spoon the mixture on to the bread, which will absorb all the oil and juices, and toss again. Serve at once.

## LETTUCE AND ARTICHOKE HEARTS
### CUORI DI LATTUGA E CARCIOFINI

*The softness of the artichoke hearts in their herby marinade and the crunchiness of the lettuce hearts results in a lovely contrast of textures in this salad. Look for the artichokes in good delicatessens. The type sold in supermarkets is often preserved in brine and is therefore not suitable.*

**TIME 10 MINUTES**

8 large artichoke hearts in olive oil marinade, drained, with olive oil reserved
4 lettuce hearts or Little Gem lettuces, separated into leaves
2 teaspoons white wine vinegar
5 tablespoons olive oil
salt and freshly milled black pepper
crusty Italian bread, to serve

**1** Arrange the artichoke hearts upright in the centre of a round serving platter.

**2** Arrange the leaves around the outside of the circle and all around the platter.

**3** Mix the vinegar, oil and salt and pepper together with any of the oil from the artichokes and drizzle this all over the leaves. Serve at once.

**Left** *Bread, tuna and basil salad*
**Right** *Lettuce and artichoke hearts*

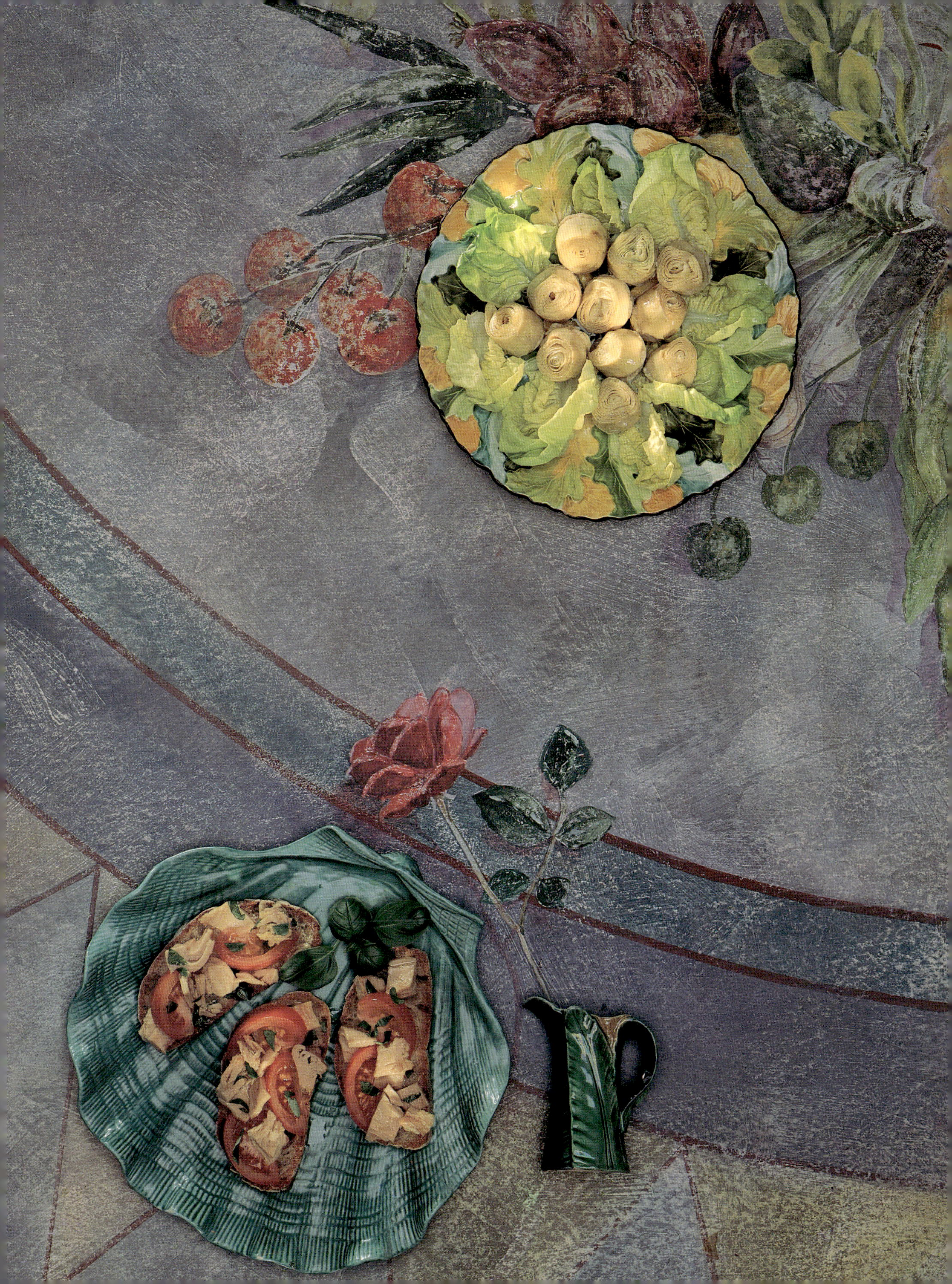

## BREAD WITH SUN-DRIED TOMATOES AND ROCKET

### PANZANELLA CON I POMODORI SECCHI E LA RUCOLA

*A delicious alternative to the more classical Tuscan* panzanella, *with a much deeper, sweeter flavour. If you can't get hold of rocket, use fresh young spinach leaves instead.*

**TIME 20 MINUTES**

**4 stale white bread rolls**
**12 sun-dried tomatoes in oil, drained, with oil reserved, and chopped**
**1 handful of fresh rocket, or young spinach leaves**
**1-2 tablespoons white wine vinegar**
**salt and freshly milled black pepper**
**olive oil**

**1** Soak the rolls in cold water for about 5-10 minutes. Take the bread out of the water and squeeze it as dry as possible in your hands. Then tear into a salad bowl.

**2** Add the tomatoes and mix them into the bread.

**3** Tear the rocket or spinach leaves into the salad and mix together again.

**4** Add the oil from the tomatoes and toss the salad. Sprinkle with the vinegar and season with salt and pepper and toss again. Add olive oil only if the salad appears to be too dry. Serve at once.

## TUSCAN BREAD SALAD

### PANZANELLA TOSCANA

*A deliciously simple summer dish which really brings out the flavour of good tomatoes.*

**TIME 15 MINUTES**

**4 stale white bread rolls**
**4 tomatoes, coarsely chopped**
**1 large red onion, coarsely chopped**
**3 tablespoons chopped fresh parsley**
**10 fresh basil leaves, torn into pieces**
**olive oil**
**salt and freshly milled black pepper**

**1** Soak the rolls in cold water for about 5-10 minutes. Take them out of the water and squeeze out the excess water with your hands. Then tear the bread into a salad bowl.

**2** Add the tomatoes and the onions and use your hands to mix all these ingredients together. Add the herbs and mix again. Dress with enough olive oil to just moisten everything and add salt and pepper to taste. Serve at once.

## MELON AND ROCKET SALAD

### INSALATA DI MELONE E RUCOLA

*This may sound like a really strange combination of flavours, but it actually works wonderfully because the sweetness of the melon contrasts perfectly with the tangy flavour of the rocket. Make sure the melon is really juicy and sweet and preferably well chilled. If you can't find rocket, tender young spinach is an acceptable alternative.*

**TIME 5 MINUTES**

1 ripe melon from which you can scoop out 400 g/14 oz of melon balls
100 g/4 oz fresh rocket leaves, picked from the stems
1 tablespoon white wine vinegar
2-3 tablespoons extra-virgin olive oil
salt and freshly milled black pepper

**1** Put all the melon balls and any melon juice in a salad bowl.

**2** In a separate bowl, mix the rocket leaves with the vinegar, oil and salt and pepper.

**3** Add the dressed rocket to the melon and toss together quickly. Serve at once.

## AVOCADO, MOZZARELLA AND SUN-DRIED TOMATO SALAD

### INSALATA DI AVOCADO, MOZZARELLA E POMODORI SECCHI

*This is a variation on the classic* insalata caprese, *a salad of tomatoes, mozzarella and fresh basil. It is very good for the winter months when fresh tomatoes have lost their intense flavour, but good mozzarella and avocados are still available.*

**TIME 10 MINUTES**

1 large mozzarella cheese or 2-3 smaller ones, thinly sliced (total dry weight 300 g/11 oz)
12 sun-dried tomatoes, with oil drained and reserved, and sliced into slivers
2 avocados, peeled and sliced
3 tablespoons olive oil
2-3 teaspoons lemon juice
salt and freshly milled black pepper
fresh basil leaves, to garnish

**1** Arrange the mozzarella on a serving dish, then scatter the slivers of tomato on top.

**2** Place the slices of avocado on top in a fan shape.

**3** Mix the reserved oil from the tomatoes with the olive oil and lemon juice. Season with salt and pepper and pour it all over the salad. Garnish with the fresh basil and serve at once.

**OVERLEAF**
**Left** *Melon and rocket salad*
**Right** *Avocado, mozzarella and sun-dried tomato salad*

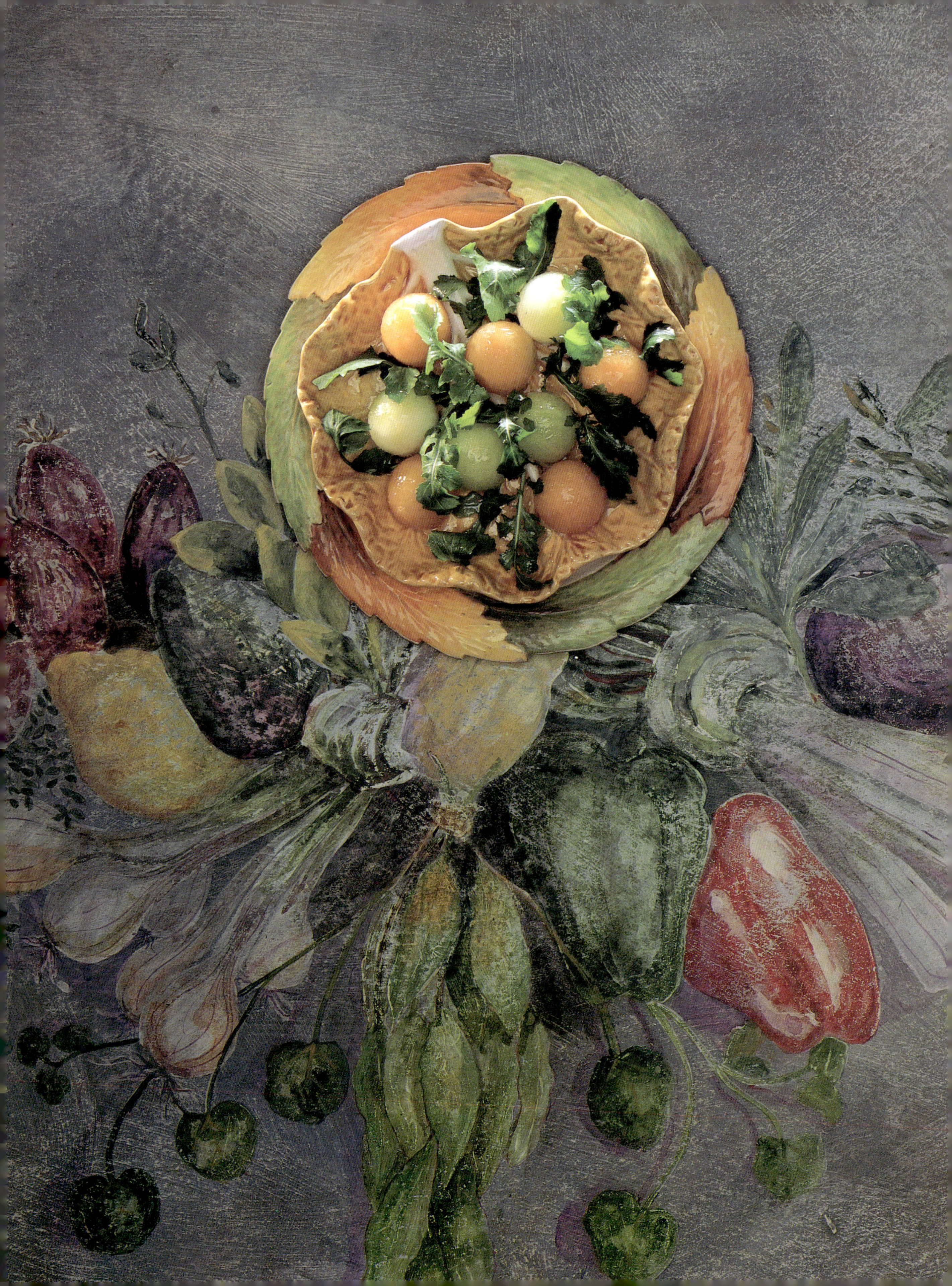

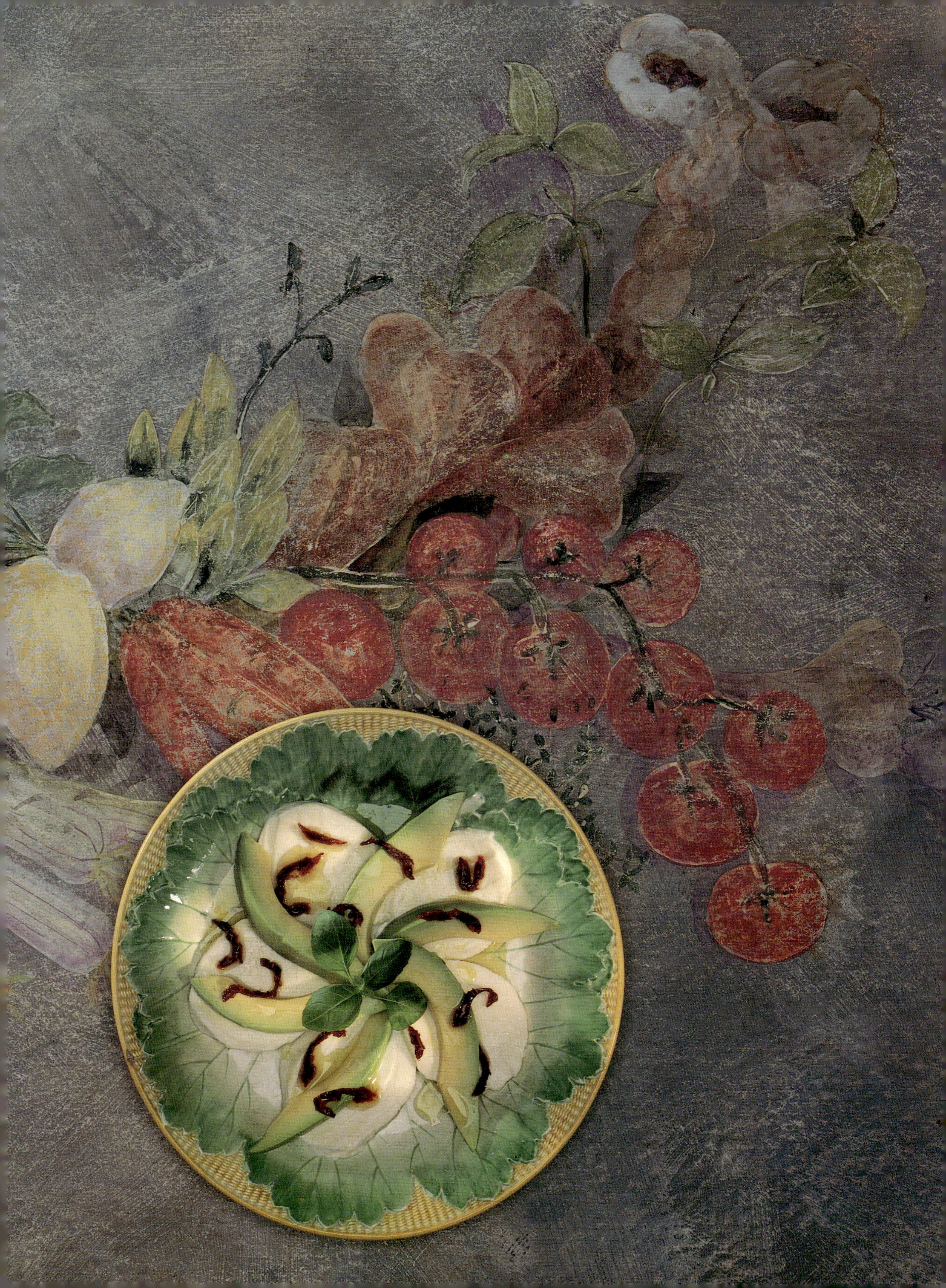

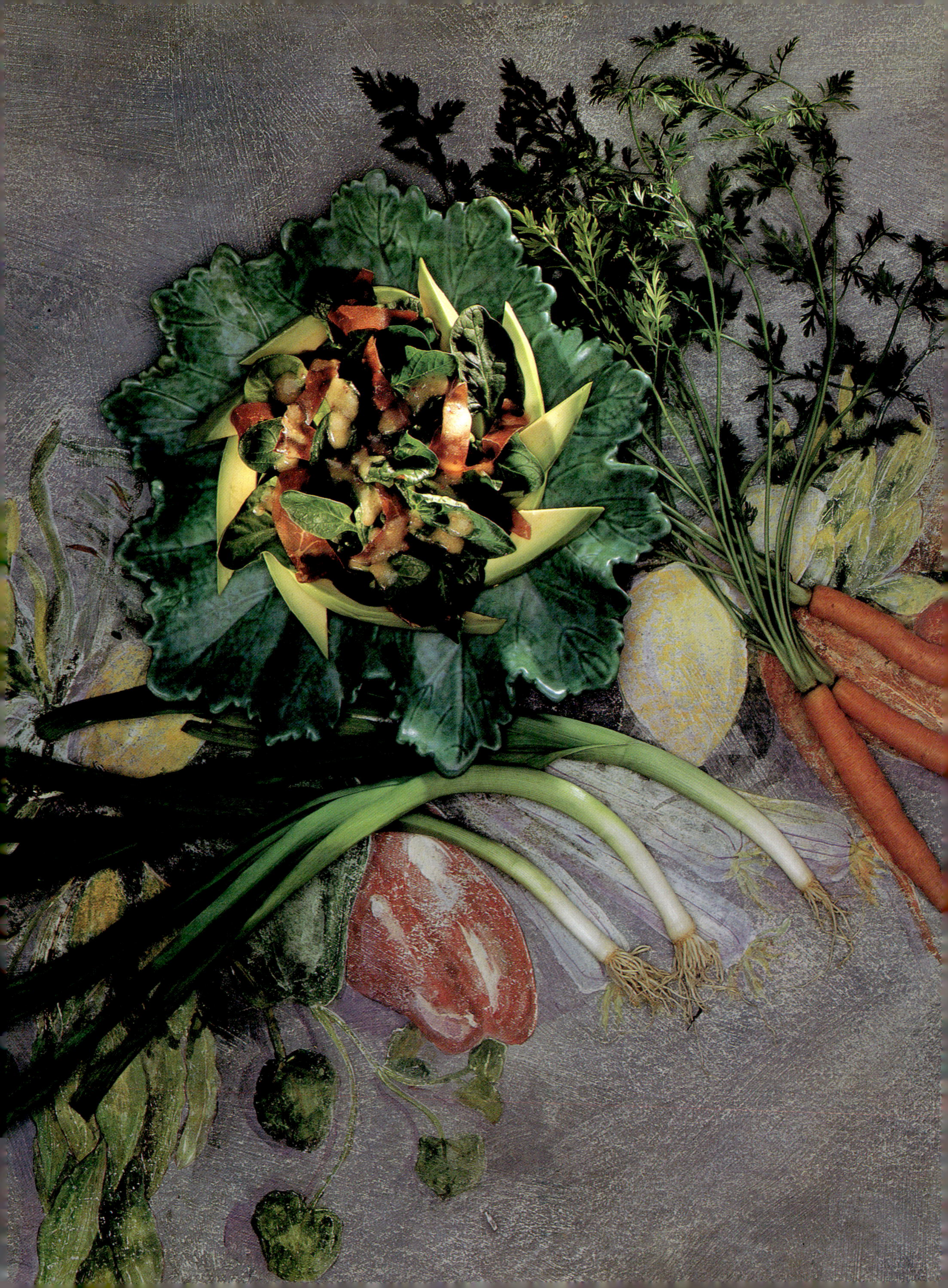

## RAW SPINACH, PROSCIUTTO AND AVOCADO SALAD

### INSALATA DI SPINACI CRUDI COL PROSCIUTTO CRUDO E L'AVOCADO

*I like the flavour combination of spinach with prosciutto crudo to add a meaty depth and then the cool smoothness of avocado. Try to choose a really strong-flavoured prosciutto, something like chamois prosciutto, wild boar or very well-matured and seasoned Parma or San Daniele. Never throw away the fat trimmings from cured meats. I keep mine in a well-sealed plastic bag in the fridge, ready for using to start off pasta sauces and risottos. This is such a marvellously quick way to add extra flavour.*

**TIME 10 MINUTES**

500 g/1 lb fresh tender young spinach, rinsed several times and picked over
8 thickish slices (knife cut) prosciutto crudo
1 large or 2 small avocado, peeled and neatly sliced
1 garlic clove, crushed to a purée
2 tablespoons red wine vinegar
salt and freshly milled black pepper
6 tablespoons olive oil
½ teaspoon whole-grain mustard
ciabatta bread or other coarse Italian bread, warmed, to serve

**1** Dry the spinach very carefully in a cloth or salad spinner. Discard the larger, coarser leaves. Arrange the remaining leaves in a salad bowl.

**2** Trim the fat off the prosciutto and reserve (see above). Cut the prosciutto into slivers. Scatter these all over the spinach.

**3** Arrange the avocado slices around the edges of the pile of spinach and prosciutto.

**4** Make a dressing by mixing the crushed garlic with the vinegar and salt and pepper. Gradually add the oil, stirring constantly, then mix in the mustard. If you are making the dressing in a jam jar, screw on the lid securely and give the jar a vigorous shake. Pour the dressing all over the salad and serve with warmed ciabatta bread.

**Raw spinach, proscuitto and avocado salad**

## POTATO SALAD WITH RED ONIONS AND ANCHOVIES

### PATATE IN INSALATA CON CIPOLLE ROSSE E ACCIUGHE

*A marvellously strong-flavoured salad that I often serve with a fairly bland-flavoured cold meat, such as pork or ham.*

**TIME 20 MINUTES**

500 g/1 lb tiny salad potatoes, well scrubbed
150 g/5 oz red salad onions, chopped
6 salted anchovies, rinsed, boned and chopped
4 tablespoons olive oil
2 tablespoons white wine vinegar
salt and freshly milled black pepper
crusty Italian bread, or grilled polenta, to serve

**1** Boil the potatoes for 10-15 minutes, until tender.

**2** Drain the potatoes and while they are still hot mix them with the onions and anchovies.

**3** Mix the oil and vinegar together and season with salt and pepper.

**4** Pour the dressing over the salad and toss together thoroughly. Serve with bread or slabs of hot grilled polenta.

## GRILLED RED PEPPER AND ANCHOVY SALAD

### INSALATA DI PEPERONI ROSSI ALLA GRIGLIA CON ALICI

**TIME 20 MINUTES**

2 red peppers, rinsed and dried
2 heads Little Gem lettuce, shredded
10 anchovies preserved in vinegar, drained with vinegar reserved, and cut into strips
olive oil
½ teaspoon anchovy paste
chopped fresh parsley, to garnish
salt and freshly milled black pepper

**1** Heat the grill to a medium heat. Grill the peppers, turning them frequently until the skins blacken and blister all over. This should take about 8 minutes.

**2** Remove the peppers from the grill and quickly rub them with a soft cloth to remove all the blackened skins. Remove whatever is left with a knife. Particularly persistent patches need to be returned to the heat for a further grilling. You will end up with slightly softer, skinned peppers. Cut them in half and remove all the seeds and the membranes. Cut into strips.

**3** Put the shredded lettuce into a shallow salad bowl. Add the pepper and the anchovy strips.

**4** Make a dressing with about 6 tablespoons olive oil mixed with the anchovy paste and reserved vinegar from the anchovies.

**5** Mix in the parsley and season with salt and pepper. Pour over the salad and toss everything together. Serve at once.

## MUSHROOM AND PARMESAN SALAD

### INSALATA DI FUNGHETTI E PARMIGIANO

*One of my favourite salads; the quantities for the dressing depend upon how much oil you like, but the most important point is that the dressing should be balanced between the oil and lemon juice and there should be enough dressing to flavour the salad without drowning it. Be sure to use just enough lemon juice to give the salad the sharpness it needs to contrast with the mushrooms.*

**TIME 5 MINUTES**

400 g/14 oz oyster or large cap mushrooms, very thinly sliced
150 g/5 oz Parmesan cheese, cut into ribbons using a potato peeler
3 tablespoons chopped fresh parsley
juice of ½-1 lemon (depending upon the size and juiciness of the lemon)
salt and freshly milled black pepper
olive oil

**1** Arrange all the mushrooms on a large serving platter. Scatter all the cheese ribbons on the top. Sprinkle with the parsley.

**2** Mix the lemon juice, salt and pepper and about 5 tablespoons of olive oil together to make a slightly sharp dressing. Pour it all over the mushrooms and cheese and serve at once.

## WARM RADICCHIO WITH PANCETTA AND PROVOLONE

### INSALATA DI RADICCHIO CON PANCETTA E PROVOLONE

*The strong, slightly bitter flavour of radicchio marries extremely well with the spicy cheese and the deliciously fatty pancetta. A really wonderful winter salad.*

**TIME 10 MINUTES**

1 very large or 2 smaller heads of radicchio
75 g/3 oz thick-cut pancetta, or strong-flavoured streaky bacon, cubed
2 tablespoons olive oil
75 g/3 oz provolone, or very mature farmhouse Cheddar, cubed
3 teaspoons balsamic vinegar
salt and freshly milled black pepper
1 tablespoon chopped fresh parsley, to garnish

**1** Shred, wash and dry the radicchio and then put it all into a shallow salad bowl.

**2** Fry the cubes of pancetta in a frying pan for about 5 minutes, until the fat is running and the cubes are crisp. Take it off the heat and stir in the olive oil, then reheat slightly for 20 seconds.

**3** Pour this hot oil and pancetta all over the radicchio, stirring to mix it in.

**4** Scatter the cubes of provolone on top and toss. Sprinkle with the vinegar, season with salt and pepper, and toss again. Sprinkle with parsley and serve at once.

**OVERLEAF**
**Left** *Mushroom and Parmesan salad*
**Right** *Warm radicchio with pancetta and provolone*

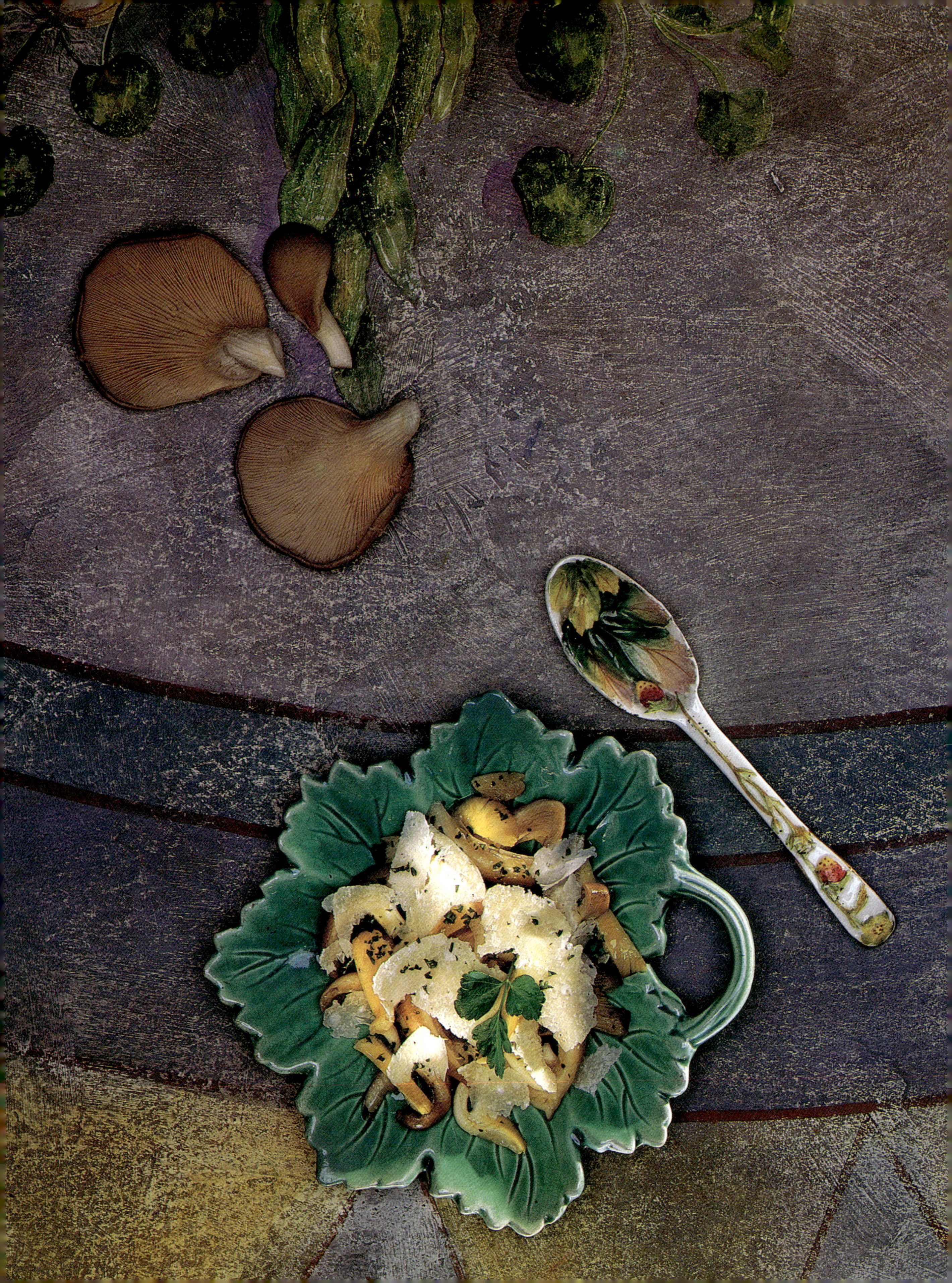

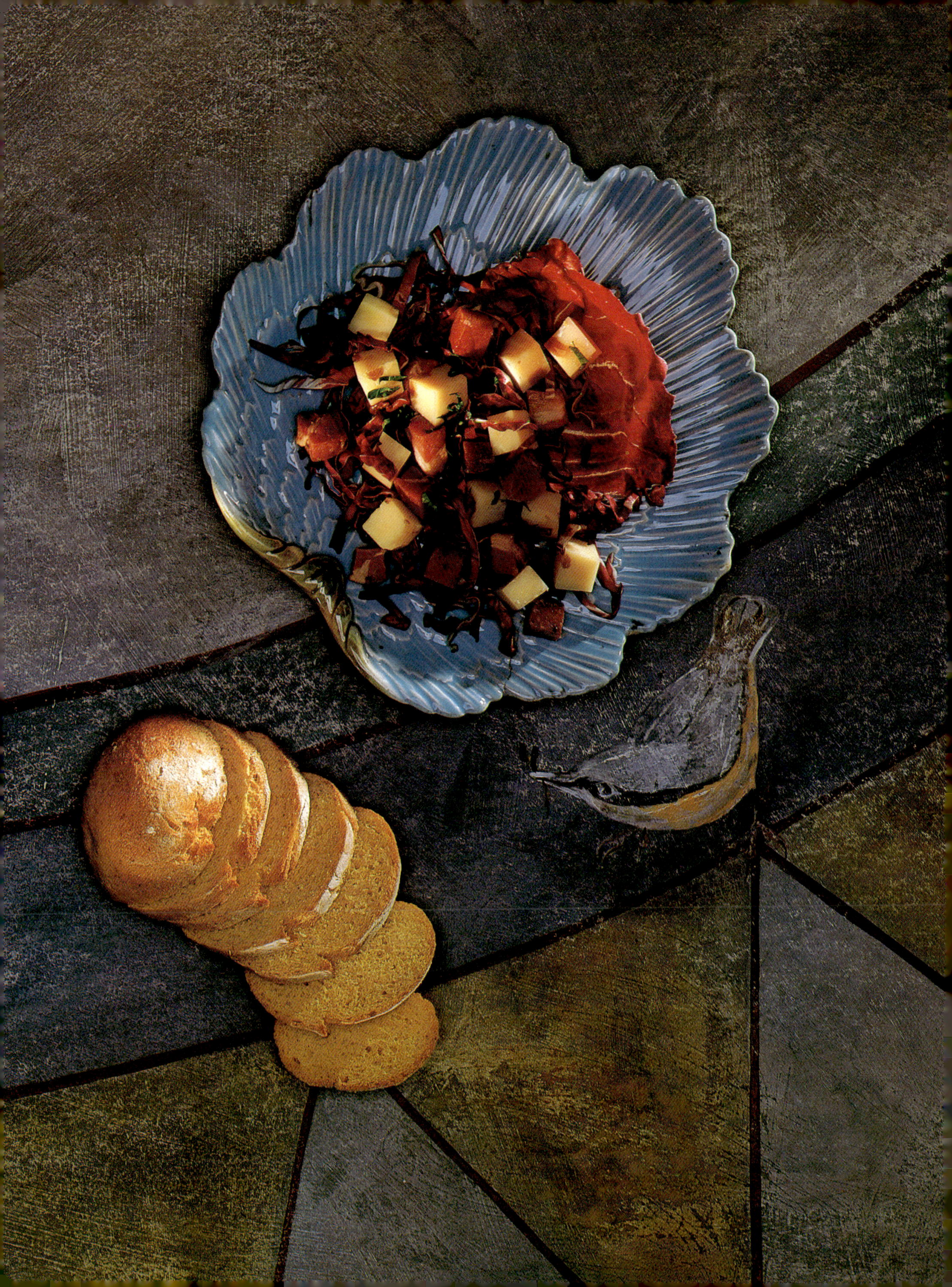

## CELERIAC AND PROSCIUTTO SALAD
### INSALATA DI SEDANO RAPA E PROSCIUTTO CRUDO

**TIME 10 MINUTES**

1 celeriac, peeled and coarsely grated
2-4 tablespoons olive oil
juice of ½ lemon
½ teaspoon caster sugar
salt and freshly milled black pepper
12 slices prosciutto crudo
small sticks of leafy celery, to garnish
crusty Italian bread, to serve

**1** Mix the celeriac with the oil (more or less of it depending upon personal taste), the lemon juice, sugar and salt and pepper.

**2** Arrange the prosciutto slices in a circle on a serving platter.

**3** Pile the celeriac in the centre of the prosciutto. Garnish with the leafy celery and serve with plenty of crusty bread.

## PROVOLONE AND MIXED LEAF SALAD
### INSALATA MISTA CON PROVOLONE

**TIME 10 MINUTES**

2 heads Little Gem lettuce, shredded
1 small head radicchio, shredded
1 handful Frisée lettuce, shredded
1 head chicory, sliced
150 g/5 oz provolone, or very mature Cheddar cheese, finely cubed
2 tablespoons red wine vinegar
½ teaspoon coarse mustard
5 tablespoons olive oil
salt and freshly milled black pepper

**1** Put all the lettuce and leaves into a salad bowl. Add the cheese cubes and mix everything together lightly so as not to bruise the leaves.

**2** Mix the red wine vinegar with the mustard, then add oil until you have about 125 ml/4 fl oz of dressing. Stir in salt and pepper to taste, then pour the dressing over the salad and toss together. Serve at once.

# SALADS 63

## RADICCHIO SALAD WITH GROVIERA
### INSALATA DI RADICCHIO CON GROVIERA

*This is a fairly filling salad, with lots of Groviera, the Italian version of Gruyère.*

**TIME 10 MINUTES**

2 heads of radicchio
250 g/8 oz Groviera (Gruyère) cheese, cut into matchstick lengths
3 tablespoons olive oil
3 tablespoons mayonnaise
1 tablespoon white wine vinegar
**salt and freshly milled black pepper**

**1** Shred the radicchio or separate it into leaves and cut the larger ones into strips.

**2** Put them in a bowl with the cheese and mix together to distribute the cheese evenly amongst the leaves.

**3** Mix the oil and mayonnaise with the vinegar to make a smooth dressing, then add salt and pepper and pour over the salad. Toss together very thoroughly. Serve at once.

## MOZZARELLA, CHERRY TOMATO AND ROCKET SALAD
### INSALATA DI MOZZARELLA, POMODORINI E RUCOLA

*A very fresh tasting salad, perfect as a light starter. If you cannot get hold of rocket, use tender young spinach leaves instead.*

**TIME 5 MINUTES**

300 g/11 oz mozzarella cheese, cubed
12 cherry tomatoes, rinsed, dried, and cut in half
75 g/3 oz rocket or tender young spinach leaves, well rinsed, picked over and dried
1½ tablespoons white wine vinegar
6 tablespoons olive oil
**salt and freshly milled black pepper**

**1** Put the cubes of mozzarella into a salad bowl. Add the tomatoes and the rocket or spinach leaves and mix the salad together.

**2** Put the vinegar and oil into a jam jar with a generous pinch each of salt and pepper. Screw on the top and shake the jar vigorously. Taste the dressing and adjust if required. Pour over the salad and toss thoroughly. Serve at once.

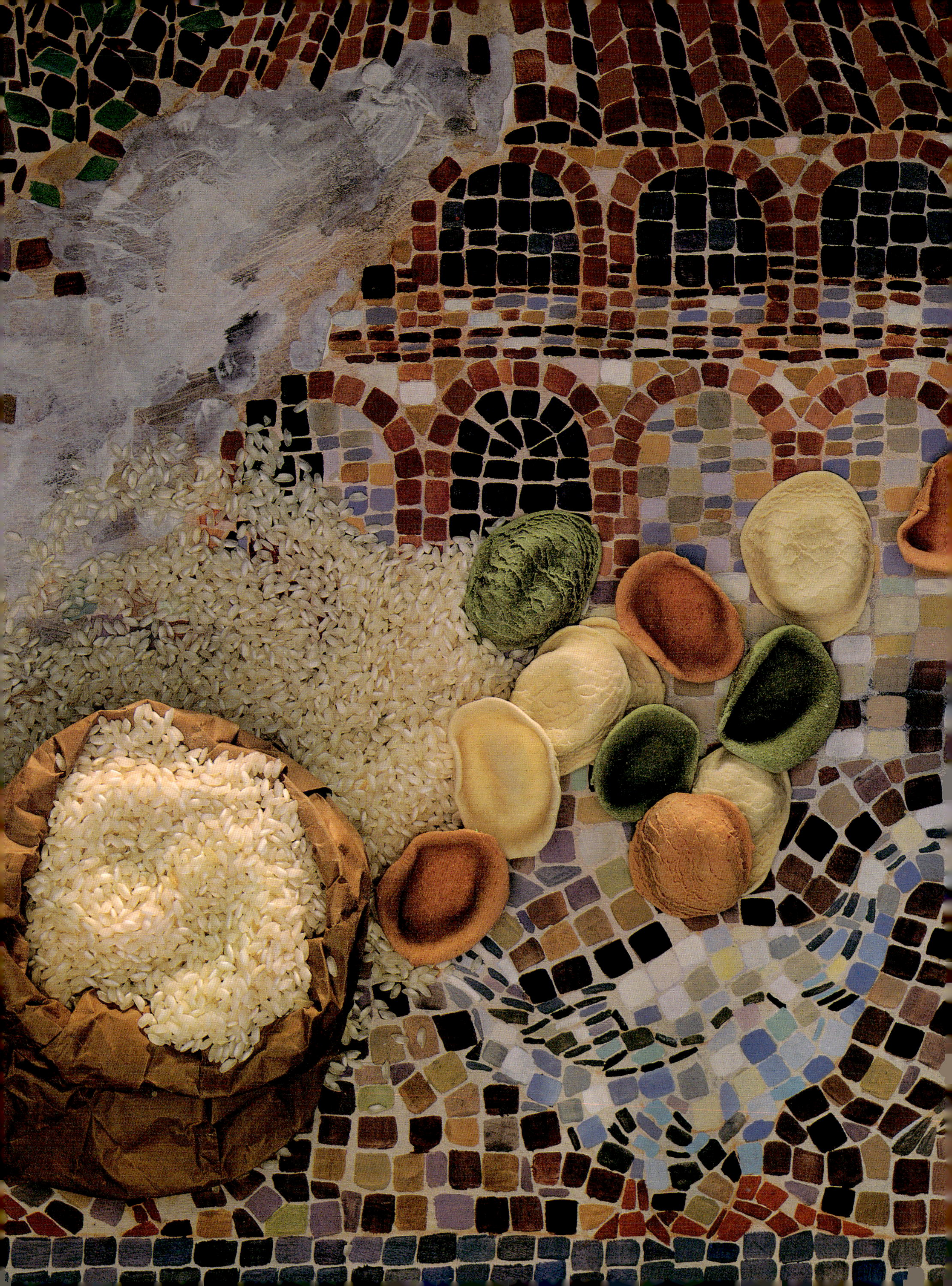

# PASTA
*and*
# RISOTTI

*Both pasta and risotti are fundamental Italian foods, versatile, healthy and offering endless flavour combinations. There are, in fact, over 650 different types of pasta on the market.*

## TAGLIOLINI WITH WALNUTS AND MASCARPONE

### TAGLIOLINI CON MASCARPONE E NOCI

*A wonderful contrast here between the soft and creamy cheese and the crunchy nuts. The hint of nutmeg gives the dish an extra depth of flavour. Fresh tagliolini take a very short time to cook, but you can use any shape or variety of pasta you like.*

**TIME 10 MINUTES WITH FRESH PASTA;
15 MINUTES WITH DRIED PASTA**

**400 g/14 oz tagliolini or spaghetti
salt
200 g/7 oz mascarpone cheese
2 tablespoons milk
½ teaspoon grated nutmeg
freshly milled black pepper
10 shelled walnuts
4 tablespoons freshly grated Parmesan cheese**

**1** Bring a large saucepan of salted water to the boil. As soon as the water boils, toss in the pasta and give it a good stir. Cover and return to the boil. Remove the lid and boil until tender.

**2** Meanwhile, mix the mascarpone cheese with the milk and the nutmeg and season lightly.

**3** Pound or process half the nuts to a fine powder and stir this into the cheese. Chop the remaining nuts coarsely.

**4** Drain the pasta, return to the saucepan and add the mascarpone mixture and the chopped walnuts. Stir everything together very thoroughly to distribute the nuts and the sauce evenly. Transfer the pasta to a warmed serving platter, sprinkle with the Parmesan cheese and serve at once.

## PAPPARDELLE WITH SPINACH AND CREAM

### PAPPARDELLE CON SPINACI E PANNA

*The flavour combination of ricotta with spinach is a classic of Italian cooking. The hint of nutmeg, Parmesan cheese and butter gives the dish a really luxurious taste.*

**TIME 20 MINUTES WITH FRESH PASTA;
25 MINUTES WITH DRIED PASTA**

**400 g/14 oz pappardelle or other wide noodle
salt
400 g/14 oz fresh spinach, well rinsed
10 tablespoons single cream
6 tablespoons freshly grated Parmesan cheese
¼ teaspoon grated nutmeg
salt and freshly milled black pepper
1 tablespoon butter**

**1** Cook the spinach for 10 minutes. Drain well, squeezing out any excess liquid, then set aside.

**2** Meanwhile, bring a large pot of salted water to a rolling boil. Toss in the pasta and give it a good stir, cover and return to the boil. Remove the lid and boil until tender.

**3** Put the cooked spinach in the food processor with the cream and Parmesan. Whizz to create a smooth green cream. Remove from the food processor and transfer to a bowl. Stir in the nutmeg and season with salt and pepper.

**4** Drain the pasta and return it to the saucepan. Add the butter and toss together thoroughly. Pour over the sauce and toss again. Transfer to a warmed serving bowl and serve at once.

*Pappardelle with spinach and cream*

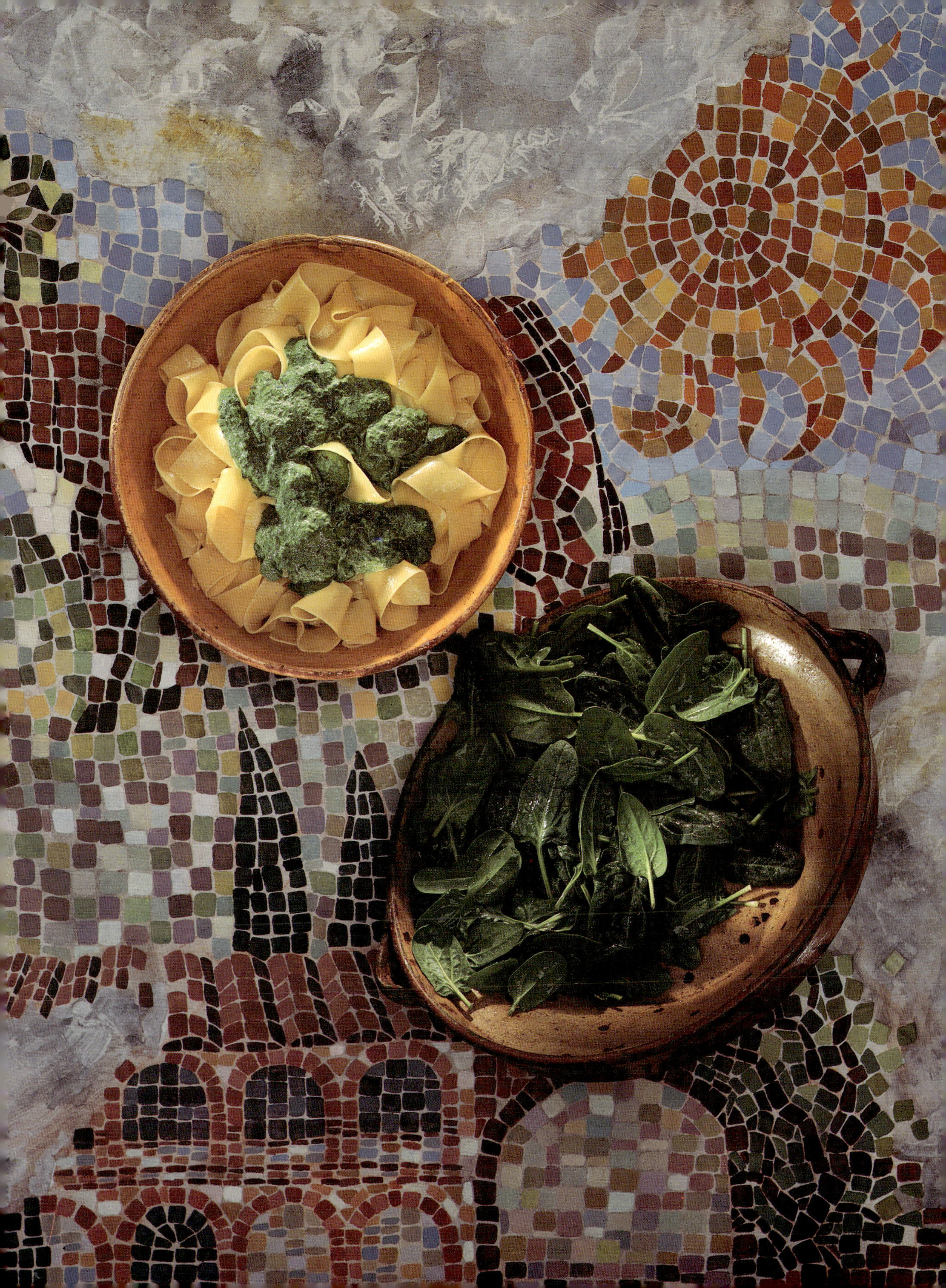

## TAGLIOLINI WITH PARMESAN, PARSLEY AND CREAM

### TAGLIOLINI CON PARMIGIANO, PREZZEMOLO E PANNA

*A delicately flavoured pasta dish that is simplicity itself. If you serve it on its own, it will make a filling starter. With salad and some Italian bread, it becomes a complete meal.*

**TIME 10 MINUTES WITH FRESH PASTA;
15 MINUTES WITH DRIED PASTA**

**400 g/14 oz tagliolini or spaghetti
salt
6 tablespoons single cream
3 tablespoons chopped fresh parsley
6 tablespoons freshly grated Parmesan cheese
freshly milled black pepper**

**1** Bring a large saucepan of salted water to a rolling boil. When the water boils, toss in the pasta, give a good stir, cover and return to the boil. Remove the lid. Boil until tender, then drain.

**2** Return the pasta to the saucepan and mix in the cream, then add the parsley and the Parmesan and mix again. Reserve a little of the parsley and the cheese to garnish the finished dish if you like.

**3** Season with as much freshly milled black pepper as you like, then transfer to a warmed platter and serve at once.

## FETTUCCINE WITH RICOTTA, PESTO AND SUN-DRIED TOMATOES

### FETTUCCINE CON RICOTTA, PESTO E POMODORI SECCHI

*I love the flavour combination of pasta with sun-dried tomatoes. In this recipe I have heightened the almost chocolaty flavour of the tomatoes with fresh ricotta as a background and then a little pesto for extra piquancy.*

**TIME 15 MINUTES WITH FRESH PASTA;
20 MINUTES WITH DRIED PASTA**

**375 g/12 oz fettuccine or other flat noodle
salt
4 heaped tablespoons fresh ricotta cheese
1½ tablespoons freshly grated Parmesan or pecorino cheese
2 tablespoons olive oil
2 tablespoons good-quality pesto
8-12 sun-dried tomatoes with oil drained and reserved, cut into thin strips
freshly milled black pepper**

**1** Bring a large saucepan of salted water to the boil. When the water boils, toss in the pasta. Give a good stir, cover and return to the boil. Remove the lid and boil until tender, stirring frequently.

**2** Meanwhile, mash the ricotta with the Parmesan.

**3** Drain the pasta, but not too thoroughly. Return it to the warm saucepan in which it was cooked. Add the ricotta and Parmesan mixture and toss together very thoroughly.

**4** Stir in the olive oil, pesto and half the sun-dried tomatoes and their oil and mix together. Add a little salt and pepper if required.

**5** Transfer to a warmed bowl, sprinkle with the remaining strips of sun-dried tomatoes and serve.

## PASTA AND BROCCOLI WITH PINE KERNELS AND CHILLI

### PASTA E BROCCOLI CON PINOLI E PEPERONCINO

*A deliciously spicy dish with plenty of crunch.*

**TIME 20 MINUTES WITH FRESH PASTA; 25 MINUTES WITH DRIED PASTA**

250 g/8 oz tiny broccoli florets
salt
400 g/14 oz pasta of your choice, such as pennette or maccheroni
4 tablespoons chilli oil
1 dried red chilli pepper
1 garlic clove, peeled and crushed lightly
1 handful of pine kernels

**1** Bring a small saucepan of lightly salted water to the boil. Add the broccoli florets and simmer for about 4 minutes or until just tender. Drain and set to one side.

**2** Bring a large saucepan of salted water to the boil. Toss in the pasta and give it a good stir. Cover the pan and return to the boil. Then remove the lid and boil until tender.

**3** Meanwhile, heat the oil in a very big frying pan with the chilli and garlic, until the oil is just starting to smoke. Discard the chilli and garlic, then add the pine kernels and broccoli and heat through, stirring frequently. Season with salt if necessary and keep warm.

**4** Drain the pasta and add it to the ingredients in the pan. Toss together very thoroughly, then transfer to a warmed serving platter and serve.

## ORECCHIETTE WITH ROCKET AND FRESH TOMATO SAUCE

### ORECCHIETTE CON RUCOLA E POMODORO CRUDO

*This dish is slightly unusual because the pasta and the herb are boiled together to make a very highly flavoured finished dish with a minimum amount of sauce. Although traditionally made with* orecchiette, *you can use any small-shaped pasta*

**TIME 10 MINUTES WITH FRESH PASTA; 15 MINUTES WITH DRIED PASTA**

400 g/14 oz orecchiette or other small-shaped pasta
salt
200 g/7 oz rocket, chopped (or spinach if unavailable)
250 g/8 oz fresh ripe tomatoes or canned tomatoes
5 tablespoons olive oil
salt and freshly milled black pepper
4 tablespoons freshly grated Parmesan cheese

**1** Bring a large saucepan of salted water to the boil, then stir in the pasta and the rocket. Reserve a few leaves of rocket to use as a garnish. Boil together, stirring frequently, until the pasta is tender.

**2** Meanwhile, peel and seed the fresh tomatoes or drain the canned tomatoes. Put the tomatoes in the food processor with the olive oil and whizz until pulpy. Season with salt and pepper.

**3** Drain the orecchiette and the cooked rocket. Return the pasta and the rocket to the pan.

**4** Pour over the tomato sauce and toss together very thoroughly. Add half the grated cheese and toss again.

**5** Transfer to a warmed serving dish, scatter the remaining raw rocket leaves and the rest of the cheese on top to garnish and serve at once.

**OVERLEAF**
Left *Pasta and broccoli with pine kernels and chilli*
Right *Orecchiette with rocket and fresh tomato sauce*

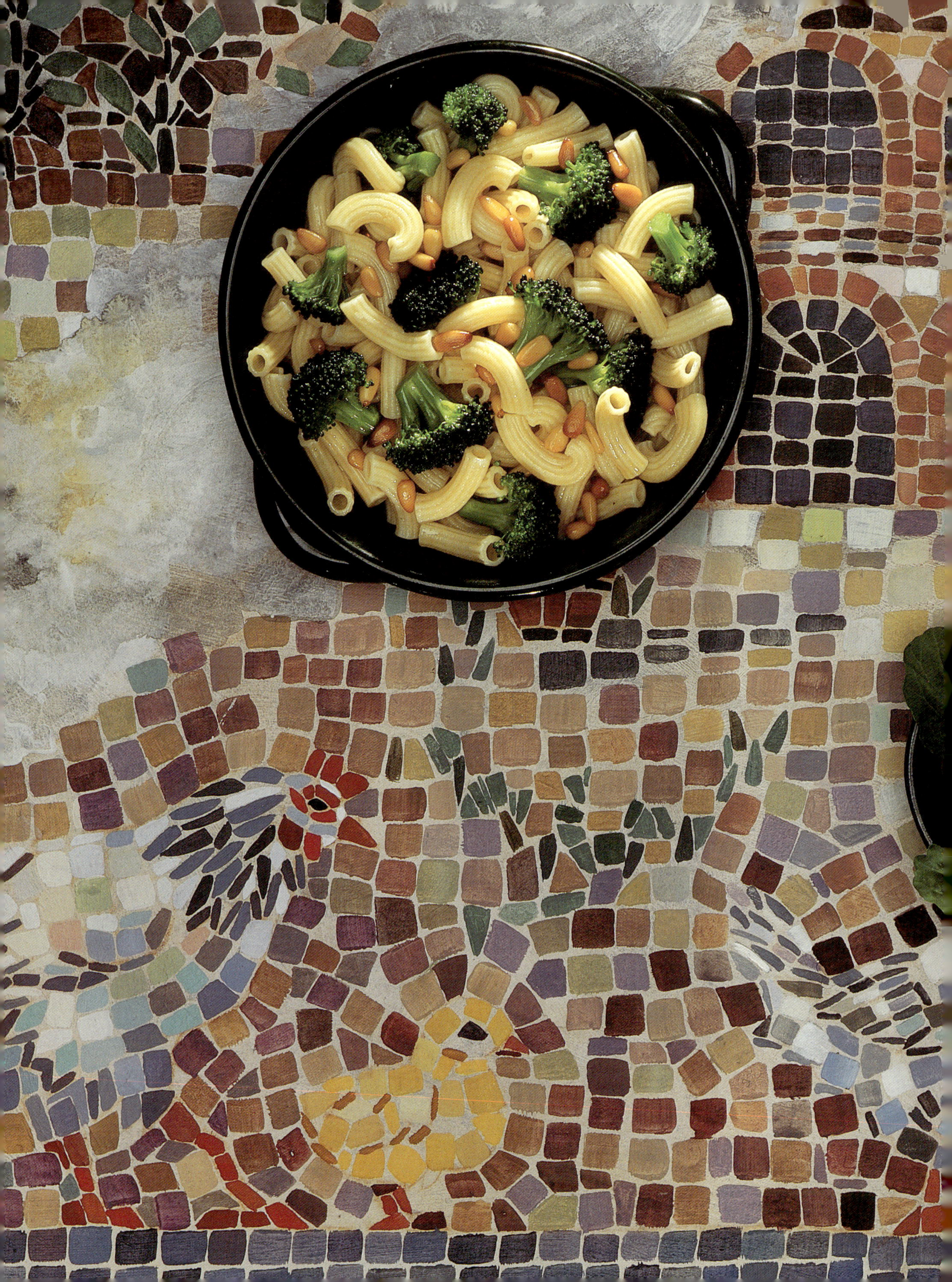

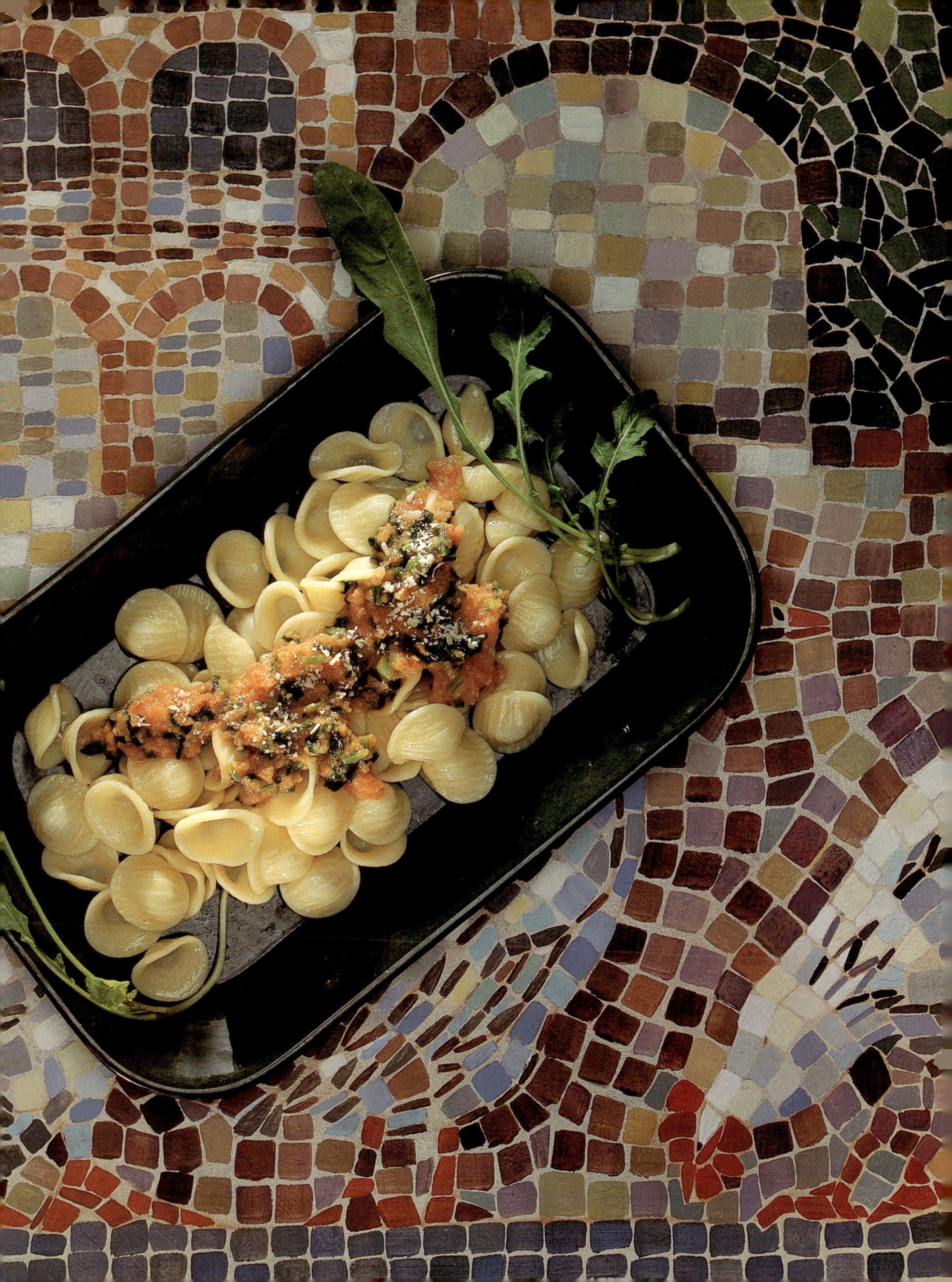

## SPAGHETTINI WITH GORGONZOLA AND SAGE SAUCE

### SPAGHETTINI CON SALSA DI GORGONZOLA E SALVIA

**TIME 10 MINUTES WITH FRESH PASTA; 15 MINUTES WITH DRIED PASTA**

**400 g/14 oz spaghettini or spaghetti**
**salt**
**200 g/7 oz Gorgonzola cheese**
**4 tablespoons milk**
**3 fresh or 2 dried sage leaves**
**freshly milled black pepper, to serve**

**1** Bring a large saucepan of salted water to the boil. Toss in the pasta and force it down into the water. Give it a stir and cover. Return to the boil, remove the lid and boil until tender.

**2** Meanwhile, cube the Gorgonzola and put it into a small saucepan with the milk and the sage. Place over a very low heat and melt the cheese, stirring frequently, until runny and smooth. Discard the sage leaves.

**3** Drain the pasta thoroughly and return to the saucepan. Pour over the melted cheese and toss together very thoroughly.

**4** Serve immediately, with freshly milled black pepper to taste.

## MILANESE BAVETTE WITH ZESTY LEMON SAUCE

### BAVETTE MILANESE AL LIMONE

*This is a very tangy, extremely light pasta dish dressed with a sauce that requires no cooking at all. You can use a combination of lemon and lime if you prefer, or even orange zest for a sweeter taste. I like to use* bavette, *but you can use any flat ribbon-shaped pasta you like.*

**TIME 10 MINUTES WITH FRESH PASTA; 15 MINUTES WITH DRIED PASTA**

**400 g/14 oz bavette or other flat noodle**
**salt**
**8 tablespoons fresh ricotta cheese**
**3 tablespoons milk**
**2 tablespoons grated lemon zest**
**juice of ½ lemon**
**2 tablespoons chopped fresh parsley**
**freshly milled black pepper**
**4 tablespoons freshly grated Parmesan cheese**

**1** Bring a large saucepan of salted water to the boil. Toss in the pasta and give it a good stir, cover with a lid and return to the boil. Remove the lid and cook until tender.

**2** Meanwhile, mash the ricotta cheese with the milk to make it creamy, then stir in the lemon zest, juice, parsley and season lightly.

**3** Drain the pasta and return to the saucepan. Pour over the sauce and toss together thoroughly. Transfer to a warmed serving dish, sprinkle with the Parmesan cheese and serve at once.

## CONCHIGLIE WITH AVOCADO AND RICOTTA SAUCE

### CONCHIGLIE CON AVOCADO E RICOTTA

*This pasta dish is dressed with a lovely pale green sauce which requires no cooking at all and is ideal for hot summer days.*

**TIME 10 MINUTES WITH FRESH PASTA; 15 MINUTES WITH DRIED PASTA**

400 g/14 oz conchiglie or pasta shells
salt
2 avocados, peeled and mashed
7 tablespoons fresh ricotta cheese
2 tablespoons milk or single cream
freshly milled black pepper
1 tablespoon chopped fresh parsley or coriander
freshly grated Parmesan cheese, to serve

**1** Bring a large saucepan of salted water to the boil. Toss in the pasta and give it a good stir. Cover with a lid and return to the boil. Remove the lid and boil until tender.

**2** Meanwhile, beat the mashed avocado with the ricotta cheese and milk or cream to make a fairly smooth sauce. Season with salt and then stir in the parsley or coriander. Finally season with plenty of black pepper.

**3** Drain the pasta and return to the saucepan. Add the green sauce and toss together thoroughly. Transfer to a warmed serving bowl and serve immediately with freshly grated Parmesan cheese.

## PASTA WITH GARLICKY OLIVE SAUCE

### PASTA CON SALSA D'OLIVE E AGLIO

*I have left it up to you to choose what shape of pasta to use in this dish, but obviously try to choose a shape that cooks quickly. I think* ruote *(wheels) work very well with this sauce. Because the sauce is cold, the dish is not piping hot, which makes it ideal for summer eating.*

**TIME 10 MINUTES WITH FRESH PASTA; 15 MINUTES WITH DRIED PASTA**

400 g/14 oz pasta wheels or other pasta
salt
15 black olives, stoned
15 green olives, stoned
2 garlic cloves, peeled
4 tablespoons olive oil
1 tablespoon soft white breadcrumbs
salt and freshly milled black pepper
1 teaspoon lemon juice
2 tablespoons chopped fresh parsley

**1** Bring a large saucepan of salted water to the boil. When it boils, toss in the pasta and give it a good stir. Cover and return to the boil. Cook until tender.

**2** Meanwhile, put the olives and garlic into the food processor and whizz, pouring in the oil gradually to make a fairly smooth paste. Add the breadcrumbs and season with salt and pepper as required. Finish off with the lemon juice. Whizz once more for just a few seconds.

**3** Drain the pasta and return to the saucepan. Pour over the olive sauce and toss together thoroughly. Add a little more oil if you think it is too dry. Transfer to a warmed serving platter, sprinkle with the parsley and serve at once.

**OVERLEAF**
Left *Conchiglie with avocado and ricotta sauce*
Right *Pasta with garlicky olive sauce*

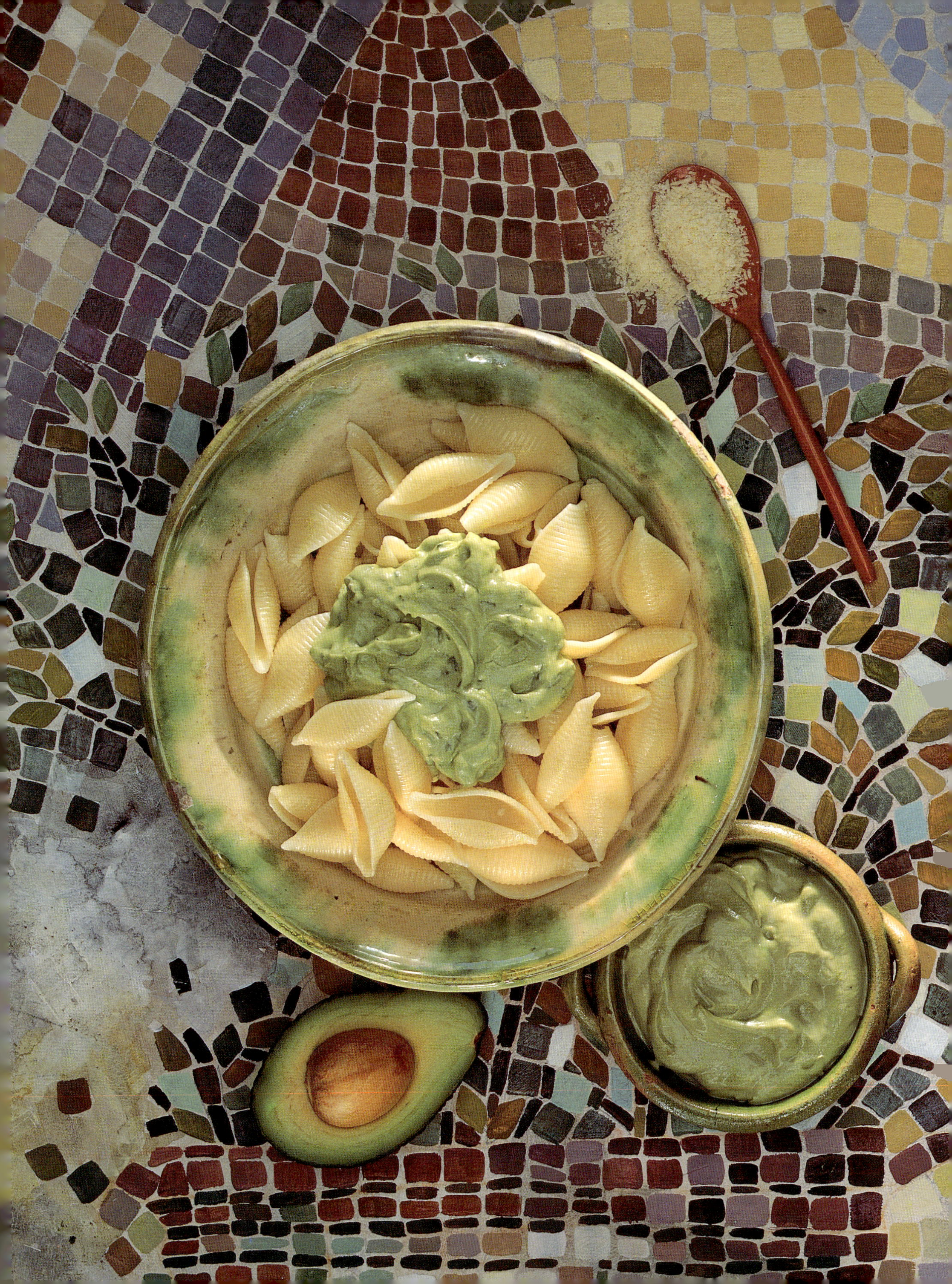

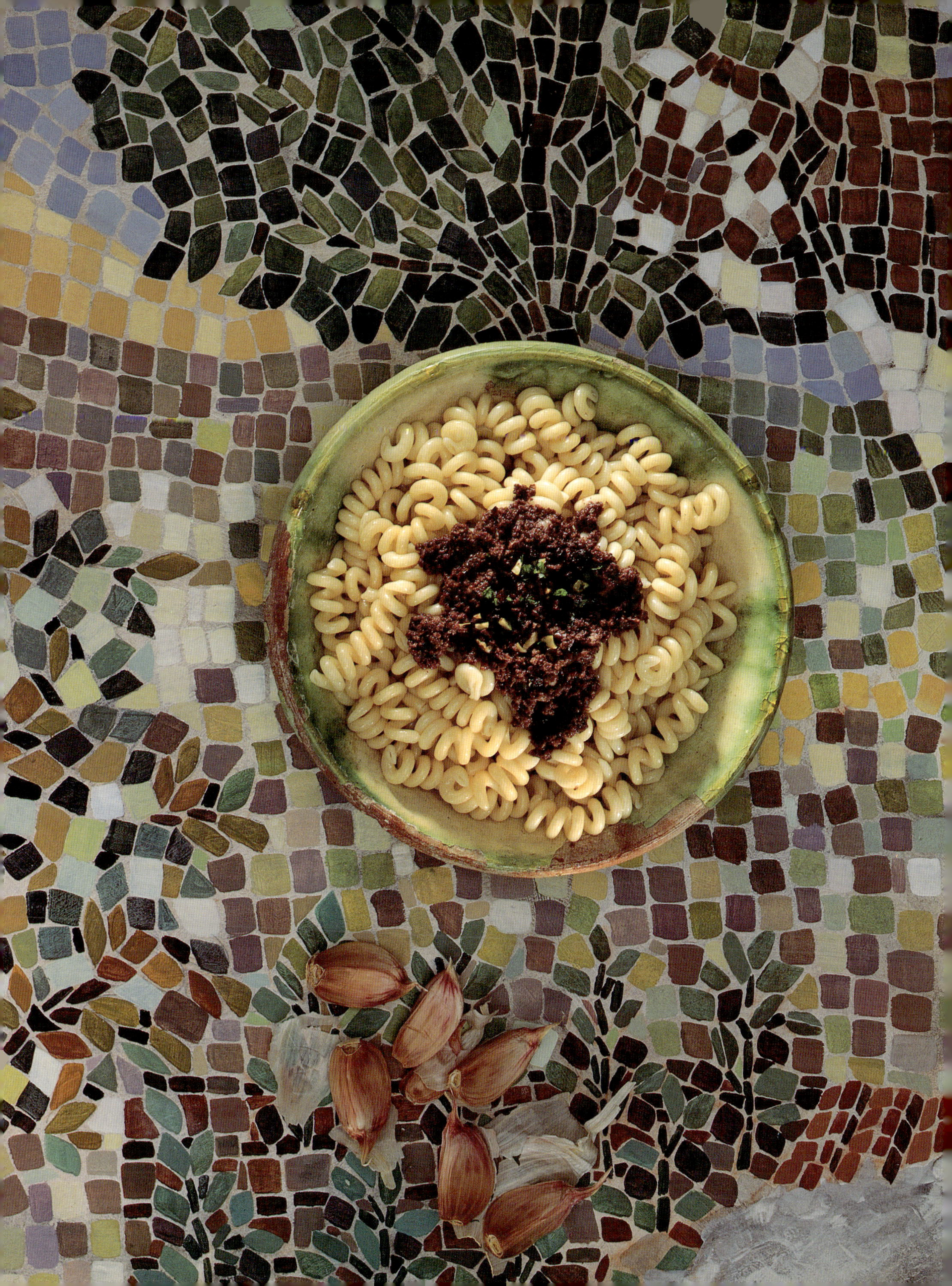

## MUSHROOM RISOTTO
### RISOTTO AL FUNGHI

*The secret for success in this very basic and simple risotto is that there should be as wide a variety as possible of different kinds of mushrooms. I like to use a selection of open-capped mushrooms with a few shiitake and oyster mushrooms and only one or two small porcini.*

**TIME 35 MINUTES**

75 g/3 oz butter
1 onion, chopped
1 garlic clove, chopped
300 g/11 oz assorted fresh mushrooms, finely chopped
300 g/11 oz risotto rice
salt and freshly milled black pepper
1½ litres/2½ pints chicken stock, kept very hot
6 tablespoons freshly grated Parmesan cheese
2 tablespoons chopped fresh parsley, to garnish

**1** Melt half the butter in a large frying pan. Fry the onion and the garlic for about 5 minutes, until soft. Add all the mushrooms and cook them, stirring, for about 5 minutes.

**2** Stir in the risotto rice and season with salt and pepper. Add the stock gradually, stirring constantly. Always wait for the liquid to be absorbed before adding anymore. After 20 minutes the rice will be soft and swollen.

**3** Take the saucepan off the heat and stir in the remaining butter and the cheese. Season with salt and pepper if necessary. Cover, and leave to rest for 2 minutes. Transfer to a warmed serving platter, garnish with the parsley and serve at once.

## COURGETTE RISOTTO WITH BASIL
### RISOTTO CON ZUCCHINE AL BASILICO

*It is important that the stock has a strong flavour, otherwise this risotto is very delicately flavoured.*

**TIME 35 MINUTES**

3 tablespoons sunflower oil
1 onion, very finely chopped
3 medium-sized courgettes, topped, tailed and very finely cubed
salt and freshly milled black pepper
400 g/14 oz risotto rice
1½ litres/2½ pints chicken or vegetable stock, kept very hot
2 tablespoons olive oil
1 handful of fresh basil leaves, torn into shreds
6 tablespoons freshly grated Parmesan cheese

**1** Heat the sunflower oil in a very large saucepan. Fry the onion and courgettes very gently in the hot oil for about 6 minutes, until the onion is soft but not coloured.

**2** Season generously with salt and pepper, then add the rice and stir thoroughly to coat the grains, then begin to add the stock gradually. Remember to wait until the rice has absorbed the liquid before adding more.

**3** After 20 minutes, when the grains are soft and swollen, take the risotto off the heat and stir in the olive oil, the basil and the cheese.

**4** Cover and leave to stand for 2 minutes, then arrange it on a warmed serving platter and serve.

## CHERRY RISOTTO

### RISOTTO DI CIGLIEGE

*A very unusual combination of flavours that actually works extremely well. The red wine enhances the flavour of the cherries enormously. You can omit the Parmesan, if you prefer.*

**TIME 30 MINUTES**

3 tablespoons butter
2 shallots, finely chopped
30 fresh dark red cherries, stoned and halved
400 g/14 oz risotto rice
salt and freshly milled black pepper
3 glasses dry red wine
1 litre/1¾ pints chicken stock, kept very hot
4 tablespoons single cream
8 tablespoons freshly grated Parmesan cheese (**optional**)

**1** Melt the butter in a large frying pan. Fry the shallots gently with the cherries for about 5 minutes, until the shallots and cherries are soft.

**2** Stir in the risotto rice, then season with salt and pepper and add half the wine. Stir constantly until the rice has absorbed all this liquid, then add the other half of the wine and stir again. Continue to cook the rice, stirring constantly and adding the stock gradually for about 20 minutes, until the rice is swollen and tender.

**3** Take the risotto off the heat and stir in the cream and, if you wish, cheese. Cover and leave to stand for about 2 minutes, then transfer to a warmed platter and serve at once.

## FENNEL AND LEMON RISOTTO

### RISOTTO CON FINOCCHI AL LIMONE

**TIME 35 MINUTES**

3 tablespoons butter
2 bulbs fennel, sliced as finely as possible
1 small onion, finely chopped
400 g/14 oz risotto rice
salt and freshly milled black pepper
1½ litres/2½ pints chicken or vegetable stock, kept very hot
2 glasses dry white wine
1 dessertspoon finely chopped fresh dill
juice of 1 lemon
1½ teaspoons grated lemon rind
7 tablespoons freshly grated Parmesan cheese

**1** Melt the butter in a large saucepan. Fry the fennel slowly with the onion and the butter for about 5 minutes.

**2** Add the rice and stir to coat all the grains.

**3** Season with salt and pepper and begin to cook the rice by adding the stock gradually and stirring constantly. After 10 minutes, stir in the wine. When this has become absorbed, add the dill and the lemon juice and rind.

**4** Continue to add liquid until the rice is swollen and soft, about a further 10 minutes. Remove the risotto from the heat. Stir in the Parmesan cheese, cover and leave for 2 minutes before serving. Transfer to a warmed serving platter and serve.

## ORANGE RISOTTO

**RISOTTO ALL'ARANCIA**

*An unusual combination of flavours, but absolutely delicious! You may not require all the stock, this quantity is just a guideline. The risotto takes 30 minutes to cook and is ready when the rice is plump and tender.*

**TIME 35 MINUTES**

**2 tablespoons butter
2 shallots, peeled and chopped very finely
400 g/14 oz risotto rice
1½ litres/2½ pints chicken stock, kept very hot
grated rind of 1 orange
juice of 2 oranges
4 tablespoons finely grated Parmesan cheese
2 tablespoons double cream
2 tablespoons chopped fresh parsley
salt and freshly milled black pepper
strips of orange zest, to garnish**

**1** Melt the butter gently in a large saucepan and fry the shallots very gently without colouring them, for about 5 minutes.

**2** Add the rice and stir constantly for about 5 minutes to coat all the grains. Add a little chicken stock to moisten the rice and allow the grains to absorb the liquid before adding any more, stirring constantly.

**3** Continue stirring and adding liquid very gradually, allowing the rice to absorb the liquid before adding any more.

**4** After 10 minutes, add the orange rind and the juice and continue to stir. Finish cooking the rice by adding liquid and stirring.

**5** After a further 10 minutes, when the grains are swollen and soft, remove from the heat, and stir in the Parmesan cheese, the cream and the parsley. Season if necessary, and cover. Leave to stand for 2 minutes, then transfer to a warmed platter to serve. Garnish with orange zest strips.

**Left** *Orange risotto*
**Right** *Fennel and lemon risotto*

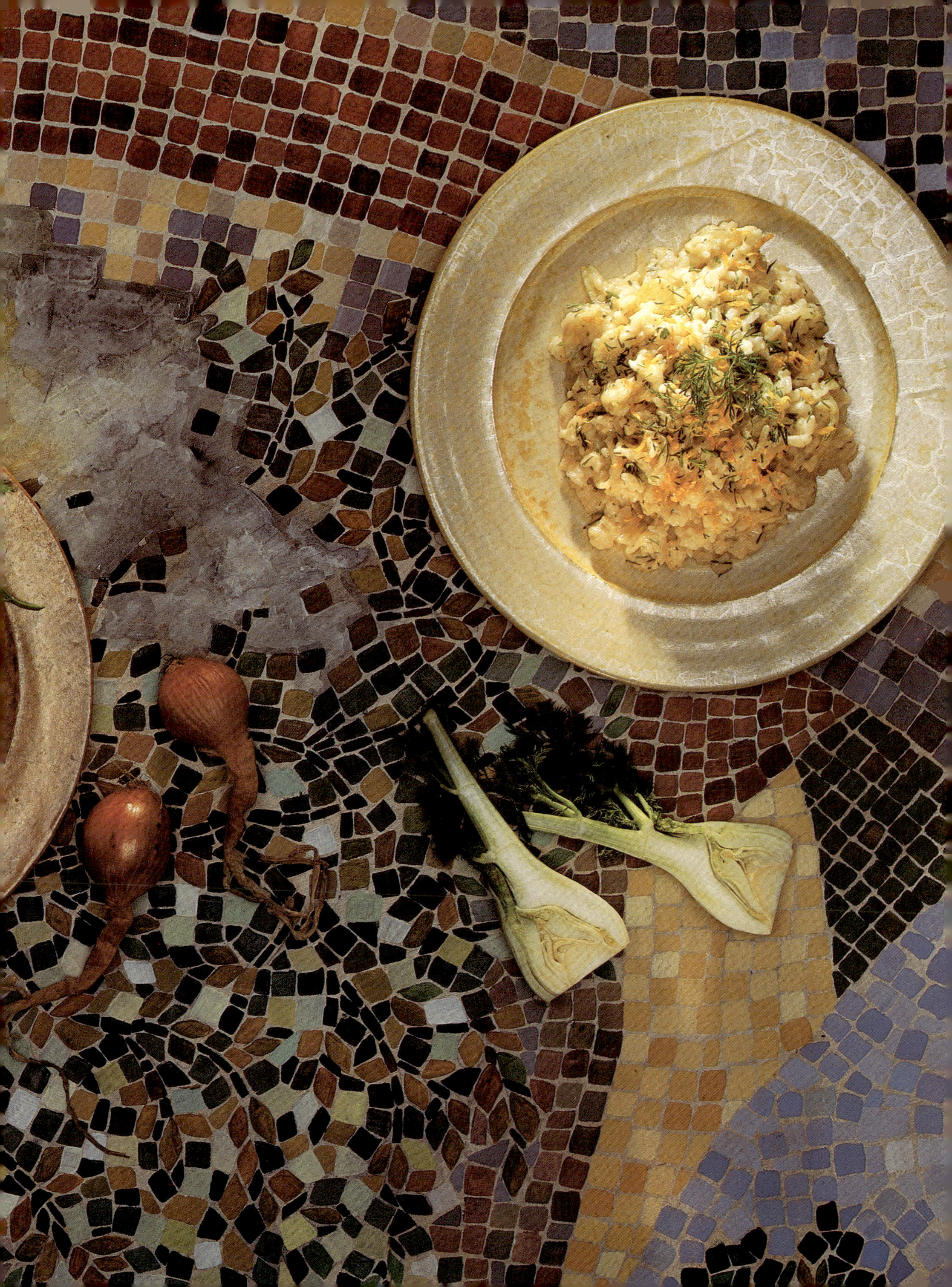

## RADICCHIO AND CREAM RISOTTO

**RISOTTO AL RADICCHIO E PANNA**

**TIME 35 MINUTES**

2 tablespoons butter
2 tablespoons sunflower oil
2 large heads of radicchio, very finely shredded
2 onions, finely chopped
3 tablespoons chopped fresh parsley
400 g/14 oz risotto rice
1½ litres/2½ pints chicken or vegetable stock, kept very hot
salt and freshly milled black pepper
4 tablespoons double cream
5 tablespoons freshly grated Parmesan cheese
4-5 fresh radicchio leaves, to garnish

**1** Melt the butter with the oil in a large saucepan. Fry the shredded radicchio and the onions together very gently for about 5 minutes or until they are soft, stirring frequently.

**2** Stir in the rice and continue cooking, adding hot stock and stirring constantly for about 20 minutes, until the grains are swollen and soft.

**3** Remove from the heat and stir in the cream and cheese. Taste and season if necessary. Cover and leave to stand for about 2 minutes. Turn out on to a warmed serving platter, garnish with the fresh leaves and serve immediately.

## RED WINE AND MUSHROOM RISOTTO

**RISOTTO AL FUNGHI AL VINO ROSSO**

*Once again, the quantity of liquid given below is only a guideline: some people like their risotto more runny than others. Remember that the risotto is cooked when the rice is plump and swollen – after 20 minutes. No further liquid needs to be added once the rice has reached the right texture.*

**TIME 35 MINUTES**

25 g/1 oz dried porcini mushrooms
1 red onion, finely chopped
3 tablespoons olive oil
300 g/11 oz button mushrooms, finely chopped
400 g/14 oz risotto rice
1 litre/1¾ pints dry red wine
500 ml/¾ pint chicken stock, kept very hot
5 tablespoons freshly grated Parmesan cheese
salt and freshly milled black pepper

**1** Put the dried mushrooms into a heatproof bowl and pour over just enough warm water to cover. Leave to soak for 10 minutes.

**2** Meanwhile, fry the red onion gently in the olive oil in a large saucepan for about 6 minutes or until soft but not coloured. Add the chopped fresh mushrooms and stir thoroughly.

**3** Drain the dried mushrooms through a muslin-lined sieve and add them to the saucepan along with the strained liquid.

**4** Add the rice and stir into the other ingredients.

**5** Pour in enough wine to cover the grains, stir thoroughly and simmer until the rice absorbs all the wine before adding anymore. Continue stirring and adding wine gradually until the rice is swollen and soft, about 20 minutes. When you run out of wine, start using the hot stock.

**6** Season the risotto with salt and pepper. Remove the risotto from the heat and stir in the Parmesan cheese. Season if necessary. Cover with a lid and leave to stand for 2 minutes. Transfer to a warmed platter and serve immediately.

## SPAGHETTINI WITH SUN-DRIED TOMATOES AND PECORINO

### SPAGHETTINI CON POMODORI SECCHI E PECORINO

*There is a marvellous contrast of flavours in this dish, between the tangy, peppery ewes' milk cheese and the soft and sweet sun-dried tomatoes, all underlined by the fiery chilli. If you cannot get hold of pecorino, use any hard grating cheese made with goats' or ewes' milk. Only use Parmesan cheese as a last resort!*

**TIME 10 MINUTES WITH FRESH PASTA; 15 MINUTES WITH DRIED PASTA**

400 g/14 oz spaghettini or spaghetti
salt
7 tablespoons olive oil
14 sun-dried tomatoes in oil, well drained with oil reserved, finely chopped
1 dried red chilli pepper
1 garlic clove, lightly crushed
6 tablespoons freshly grated pecorino cheese

**1** Bring a large saucepan of salted water to the boil. As soon as the water boils, toss in the pasta and force it down into the water. Give it a good stir and then cover. Return to the boil, then remove the lid and boil until tender.

**2** Meanwhile, heat the olive oil and the oil reserved from the tomatoes in a smaller saucepan with the chilli and garlic for about 2 minutes or until the garlic is soft, stirring frequently, then discard the chilli and garlic.

**3** Drain the pasta, return to the saucepan and pour over the warm oil. Toss together, then add the tomatoes and toss again.

**4** Add half the cheese and toss once more before transferring to a warmed serving platter. Sprinkle with the remaining cheese and serve at once.

## LEEK AND PUMPKIN RISOTTO

### RISOTTO CON I PORRI E LA ZUCCA

*When pumpkin is not in season, use peeled and cubed aubergine instead. If using aubergine, it will need to be salted and left to stand under a weight in a colander to release its bitter juices.*

**TIME 35 MINUTES**

3 tablespoons butter
2 small leeks, well rinsed, trimmed and finely chopped
200 g/7 oz pumpkin or aubergine flesh, very finely cubed
400 g/14 oz risotto rice
1½ litres/2½ pints chicken or vegetable stock, kept very hot
salt and freshly milled black pepper
8 tablespoons freshly grated Parmesan cheese

**1** Melt the butter in a large saucepan. Fry the leeks for about 5 minutes until soft but not coloured. Then add the pumpkin and fry gently, stirring, for about 5 minutes.

**2** Stir in the rice, then begin to add the stock a little at a time, stirring constantly. Season with salt and pepper and continue to add stock and stir for 20 minutes, until the grains are swollen and soft.

**3** Take the risotto off the heat and stir in the cheese. Cover and leave to stand for 2 minutes, then transfer to a warmed serving platter and serve.

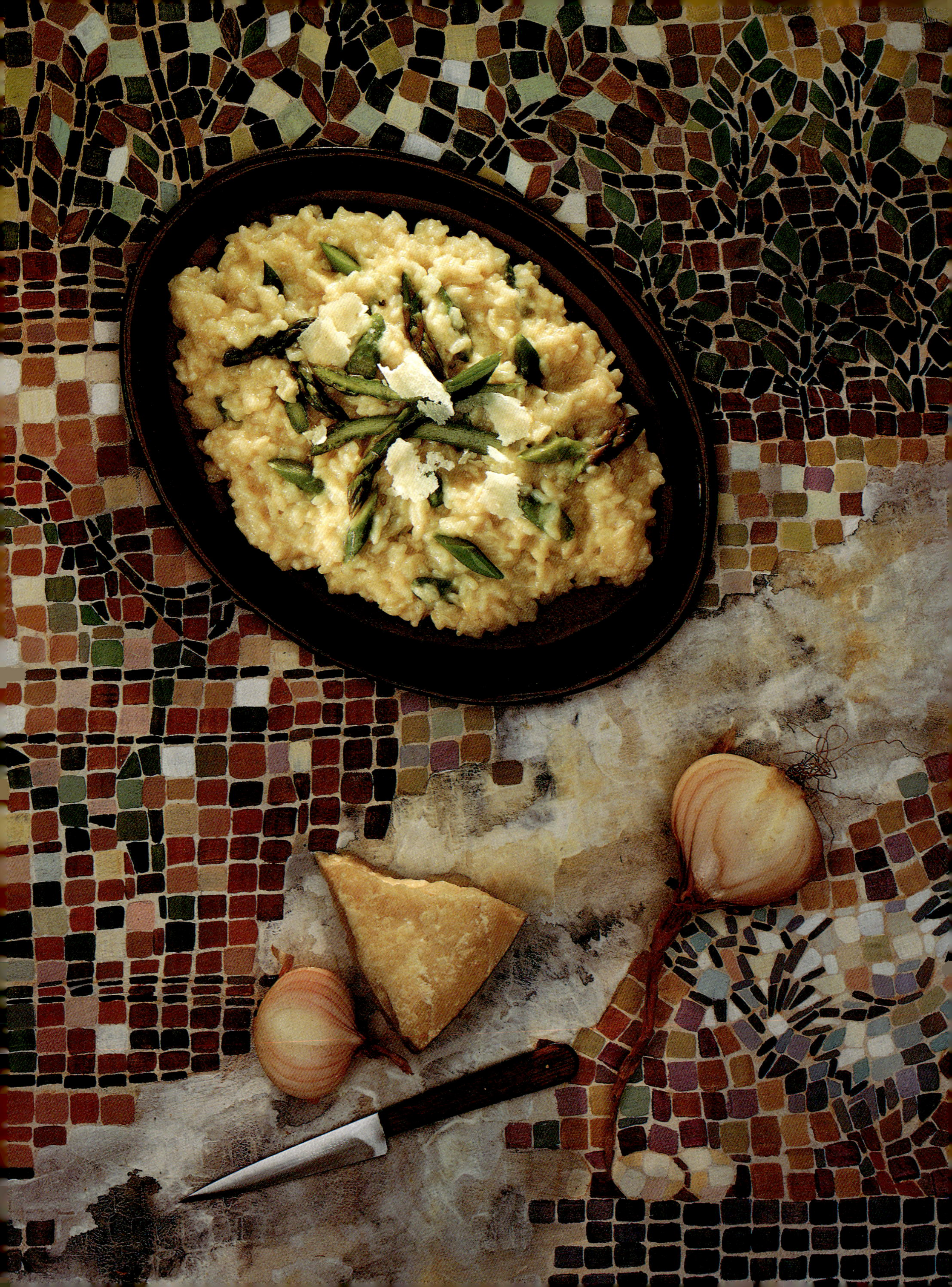

## ASPARAGUS RISOTTO

### RISOTTO D'ASPARAGI

*One of the more common varieties of risotto for which you can use fresh or frozen asparagus. I do not, however, recommend using the canned variety.*

**TIME 35 MINUTES**

300 g/11 oz asparagus spears, fresh or frozen
75 g/3 oz butter
1 onion, very finely chopped
400 g/14 oz risotto rice
salt and freshly milled black pepper
1 large glass dry white wine
1½ litres/2½ pints chicken stock, kept very hot
7 tablespoons freshly grated Parmesan cheese

**1** Slice the asparagus spears on the diagonal, reserving one for the garnish.

**2** Melt half the butter in a very large frying pan. Fry the onion very gently with the asparagus spears for about 8 minutes.

**3** Stir in the rice, then season with salt and pepper. Gradually add the wine and allow the liquid to be absorbed before adding more. Then add the stock very gradually, stirring constantly, until the grains are soft and swollen, about 20 minutes.

**4** Remove the risotto from the heat and stir in the cheese and remaining butter. Season with salt and pepper if necessary. Cover and leave to rest for 2 minutes. Transfer to a warmed platter, garnish with thin slivers of asparagus and serve at once.

## PEA AND BACON RISOTTO

### RISOTTO DI PISELLINI E PANCETTA

**TIME 35 MINUTES**

3 tablespoons sunflower oil
1 large onion, finely chopped
8 rashers streaky bacon or pancetta, rinded if necessary and chopped
400 g/14 oz risotto rice
150 g/5 oz frozen petits pois
500 ml/¾ pint full-bodied dry white wine
1 litre/1¾ pints chicken stock, kept hot (you may not use it all)
salt and freshly milled black pepper
8 tablespoons freshly grated Parmesan cheese
1 walnut-sized knob of butter

**1** Heat the oil in a large saucepan. Fry the onion gently in the sunflower oil for about 5 minutes, or until soft.

**2** Stir in the bacon, rice and peas and enough wine to just cover the grains. Stir until the rice has absorbed the liquid, then add more and continue stirring, until all the wine is absorbed.

**3** Begin adding the stock, and continue, stirring constantly for about 20 minutes, until the grains are swollen and soft.

**4** Remove from the heat, stir in the Parmesan and the butter, season with salt and pepper, cover and rest for 2 minutes. Pour it out on to a warmed platter and serve immediately.

*Asparagus risotto*

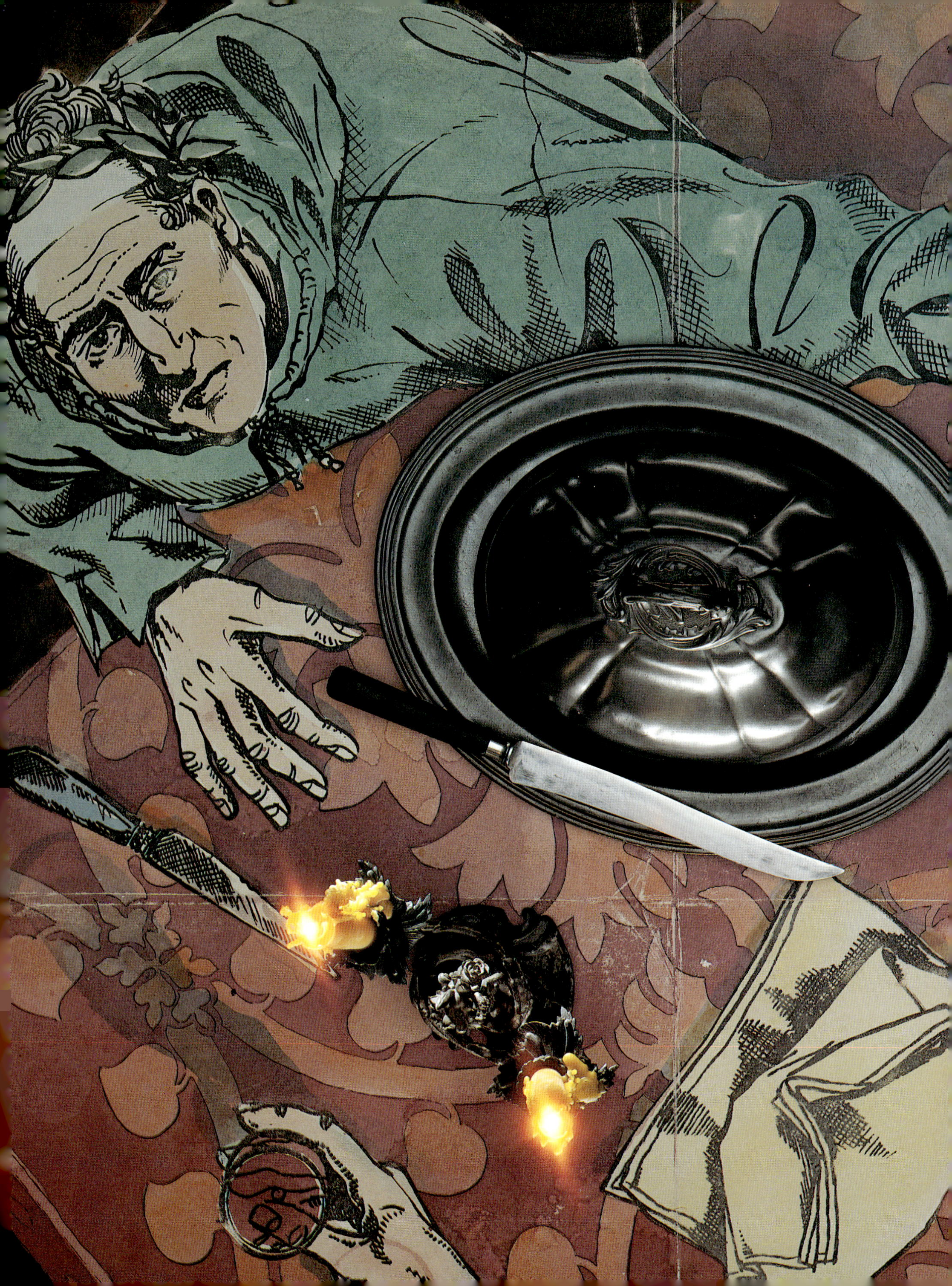

# MEAT
*and*
# POULTRY

*Today, meat in Italy is cooked much more lightly and simply than it used to be, which calls for leaner and more succulent cuts of meat.*

## VEAL SCALOPPINE WITH MARSALA
### SCALOPPINE DI VITELLO AL MARSALA

*An extraordinarily classical dish, which never seems to date.*

**TIME 15 MINUTES**

**4 veal or turkey escalopes, each weighing about 175 g/6 oz, well trimmed**
**1½ tablespoons plain white flour**
**salt and freshly milled black pepper**
**2 tablespoons unsalted butter**
**4 tablespoons Marsala**

**1** Flatten the meat as much as possible with a meat mallet or the side of a large knife. Cut it into small, even-sized pieces, about 7.5 cm/3 in square.

**2** Put the flour and some salt and pepper into a plastic bag. Add the meat and shake it around to coat it completely. Remove the meat and shake off any excess.

**3** Melt the butter in a large frying pan until foaming lightly, then lay the meat in the pan and seal it on both sides. Fry it gently in the butter for 3-4 minutes, until golden brown.

**4** Remove the meat from the pan and arrange it on a very hot serving platter to keep it warm. Pour the Marsala into the pan and stir it around very thoroughly, scraping the botttom of the pan to remove any of the flour that may have stuck. Pour the sauce all over the meat, and serve at once.

## MINUTE STEAK WITH GARLIC AND TOMATO
### BISTECCHINA ALL'AGLIO E POMODORO

*This is the classic* pizzaiola, *made with beef and using* passata—*sieved and puréed canned tomatoes—for a very speedy dish.*

**TIME 10 MINUTES**

**4 minute steaks, each weighing about 175 g/6 oz, trimmed and flattened with a meat mallet**
**3 tablespoons olive oil**
**3 garlic cloves, chopped**
**8 tablespoons passata**
**salt and freshly milled black pepper**
**chopped fresh parsley, to garnish**

**1** Make sure the meat is trimmed of fat and flattened evenly.

**2** Heat the olive oil in a large frying pan and fry the garlic for about 3 minutes, until golden brown.

**3** Stir in the passata and season generously with salt and pepper.

**4** Slide the meat into the sauce and cook together quickly for about 4 minutes.

**5** Transfer to a warmed serving dish. Garnish with chopped parsley and serve at once.

## MINI MEATBALLS ON A BED OF LEAVES
### POLPETTINE CON L'INSALATA

*A deliciously light and pretty dish. The meatballs are also wonderful cold.*

**TIME 15 MINUTES • MAKES 12 SMALL MEATBALLS**

sunflower oil for deep frying
2 chicken breasts, each weighing about
   175 g/6 oz, skins removed, and finely minced
grated rind of ½ lemon
2 tablespoons chopped fresh parsley
3 tablespoons soft white breadcrumbs
2 eggs
salt and freshly milled black pepper
2 tablespoons plain white flour
3 tablespoons dried white breadcrumbs
1 head Lollo Rosso lettuce, rinsed, dried and
   torn into pieces
4 sprigs Lamb's lettuce, rinsed and dried
4 leaves Cos lettuce, rinsed, dried and torn
   into pieces
3 sprigs rocket, rinsed and dried
8 fresh basil leaves, rinsed and dried
3 tablespoons olive oil
1 teaspoon white wine vinegar
lemon wedges, to garnish

**1** Heat the oil in a deep saucepan or a deep fat fryer until sizzling hot.

**2** Meanwhile, mix together the minced chicken, the lemon rind, parsley, soft breadcrumbs and 1 egg. If you feel this mixture is too dry, add a little water. Season with salt and pepper and form this mixture into small spheres the size of golf balls.

**3** Toss the meatballs in flour, in a plastic bag. Remove and shake off any excess flour. Beat the second egg and use it to coat the meatballs, then cover them in dried breadcrumbs.

**4** Fry the meatballs until crisp and golden, frying in batches if necessary. Drain thoroughly on kitchen paper and keep warm.

**5** Toss all the leaves together in a salad bowl. Mix together the oil and vinegar and salt and pepper. Pour this over the salad and toss together.

**6** Arrange the salad on a large serving dish and put the meatballs on top. Garnish with lemon wedges.

## LAMB CHOPS WITH CHILLI SAUCE
### BRACIOLETTE D'AGNELLO CON IL PEPERONCINO

*These simple grilled lamb chops, coated with a spicy tomato sauce, are ideal for a quick tasty meal. The sauce can be cooked in the time it takes to grill the meat.*

**TIME 12 MINUTES**

2 tablespoons olive oil
2 garlic cloves, chopped
1 dried red chilli pepper, rubbed lightly
   in your palms
9 tablespoons passata
salt and freshly milled black pepper
4 chump lamb chops, each weighing about
   175 g/6 oz, trimmed of as much fat as possible
fresh mint sprigs, to garnish

**1** Heat the grill to medium.

**2** Heat the olive oil in a large frying pan and cook the garlic and chilli until the garlic is golden.

**3** Stir in the passata. Season with salt and pepper and leave to simmer while the meat cooks.

**4** Grill the chops for about 4 minutes on each side or until just pink in the middle.

**5** Remove the chilli from the sauce. Arrange the meat on a serving platter, cover with the sauce, garnish with the mint and serve at once.

**OVERLEAF**
**Left** *Mini meatballs on a bed of leaves*
**Right** *Minute steak with garlic and tomato*

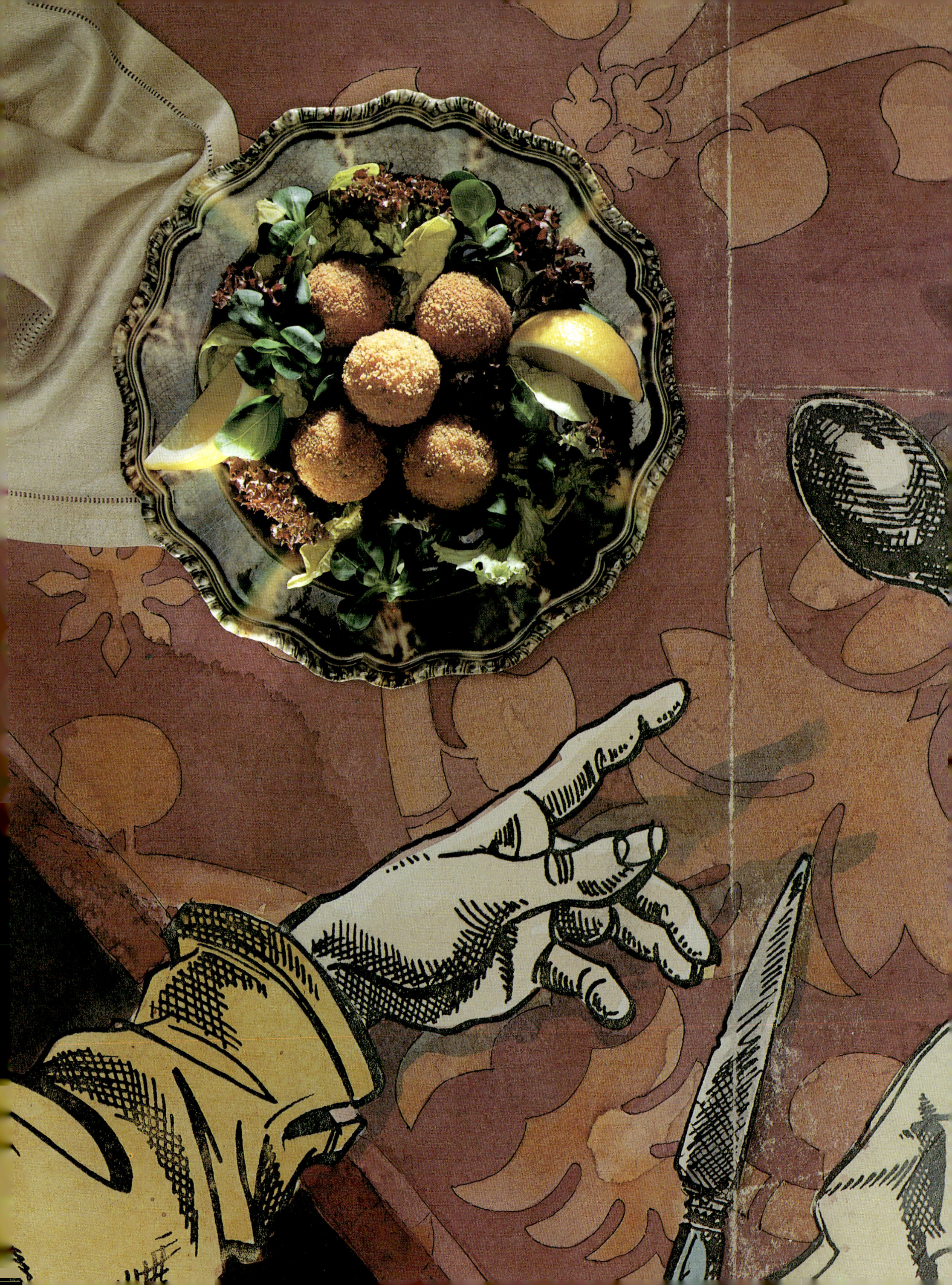

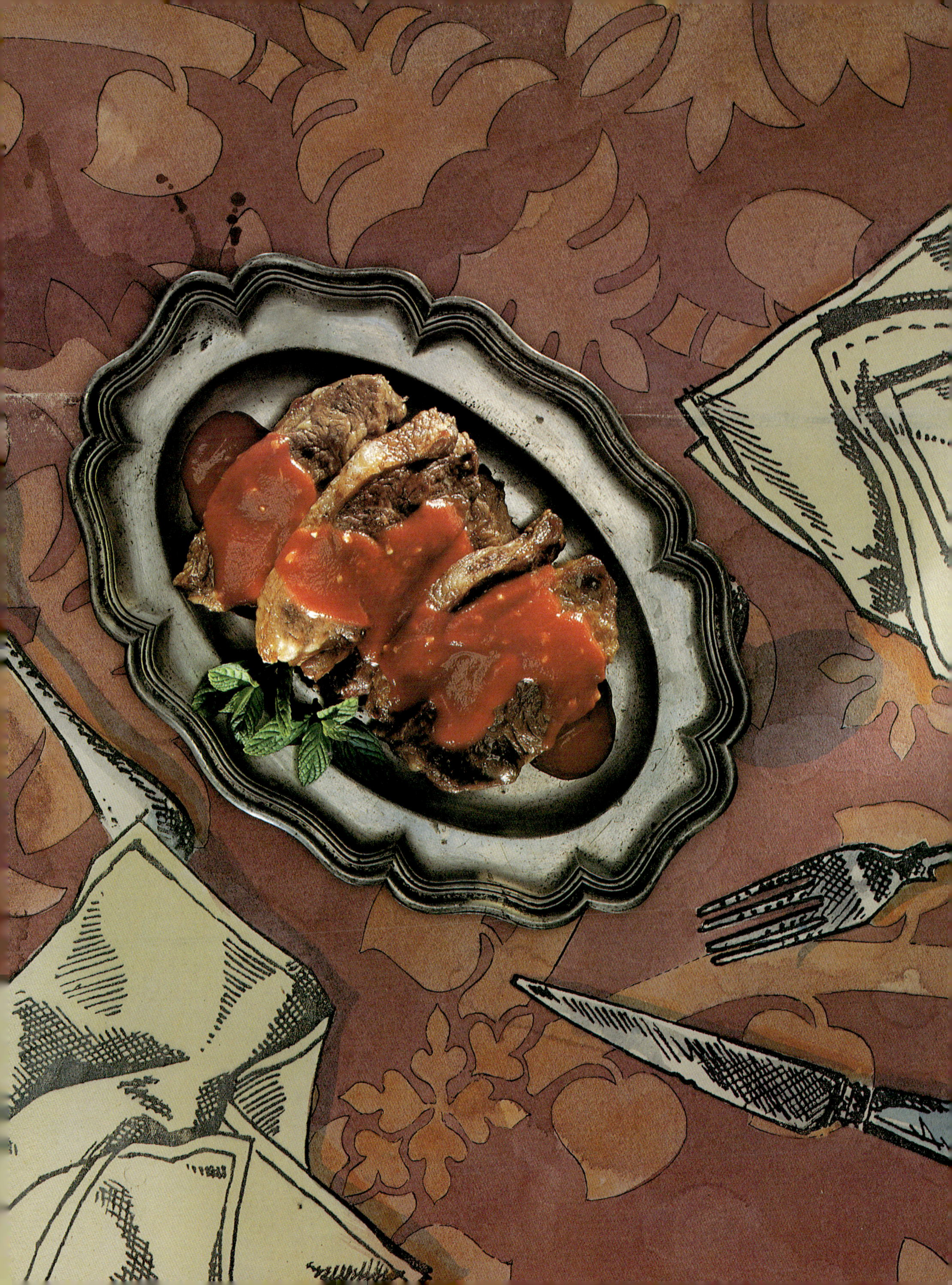

## CHICKEN BREASTS WITH LEMON AND ROSEMARY

### PETTI DI POLLO COL LIMONE E ROSMARINO

*A succulent and fresh tasting way to serve chicken breasts. Real rosemary lovers can add as much of this pungent herb as they wish. Always try to use fresh rosemary rather than dried if you can.*

**TIME 25 MINUTES**

4 boned chicken breasts, each weighing about 175 g/6 oz, skins removed
1 tablespoon plain white flour
salt and freshly milled black pepper
3 tablespoons olive oil
1 sprig fresh rosemary, approximately 10 cm/4 in long
grated rind of ½ lemon
juice of ½ lemon
sliced rind of ½ lemon, to garnish
fresh rosemary, to garnish

**1** Flatten the chicken breasts lightly with a meat mallet or the side of a very heavy knife. Cut them in half and trim them up so that they look neat.

**2** Mix the flour with a pinch of salt and a little pepper. Coat the chicken breasts lightly with the seasoned flour, shaking off any excess.

**3** Heat the oil with the rosemary in a large frying pan over a very low heat for about 3 minutes.

**4** Raise the heat and brown the chicken breasts for about 3 minutes on each side. Add the grated lemon rind and pour over the lemon juice. Cook over a medium heat for about 10 minutes or so, turning the breasts over frequently until all the juices run clear when tested with the tip of a knife.

**5** Transfer to a warm serving dish, garnish with the lemon rind and fresh rosemary and serve.

## TURKEY BREASTS WITH PROSCIUTTO AND MELTED CHEESE

### PETTI DI TACCHINO CON PROSCIUTTO E FORMAGGIO

*This is a very simple and much lighter version of the classic Roman dish called* saltimbocca. *Olive oil may be used instead of butter, if prefered.*

**TIME 15 MINUTES**

8 very thin turkey breasts, each weighing about 100 g/4 oz, trimmed
1 tablespoon plain white flour
salt and freshly milled black pepper
2 tablespoons butter
8 very thin slices prosciutto crudo, most of fat removed
8 very thin slices of mozzarella cheese
chopped fresh parsley, to garnish

**1** Flatten the turkey breasts as much as possible with a meat mallet or the side of a very heavy knife. Then trim each fillet to make them of even size.

**2** Coat the breasts very lightly with flour and season with a little salt and pepper.

**3** Melt the butter in a large frying pan with a lid and seal the turkey on both sides in the butter.

**4** Cover each breast with a slice of prosciutto and then lay a slice of mozzarella on top.

**5** Cover the pan with a lid, raise the heat and heat through for about 2 minutes, just long enough for the cheese to melt slightly. Transfer to a warmed serving dish and sprinkle with the parsley just before serving.

*Turkey breasts with proscuitto and melted cheese*

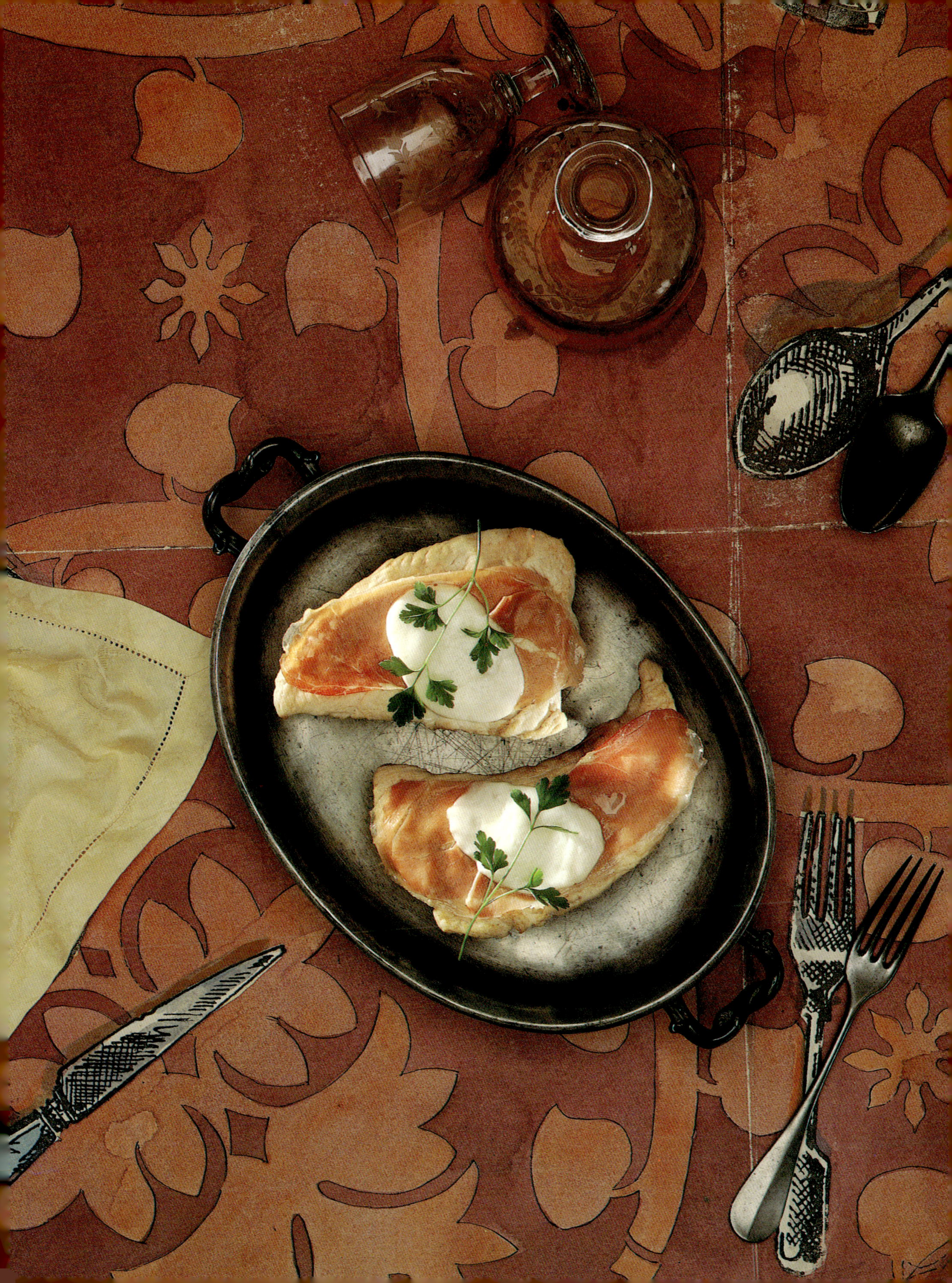

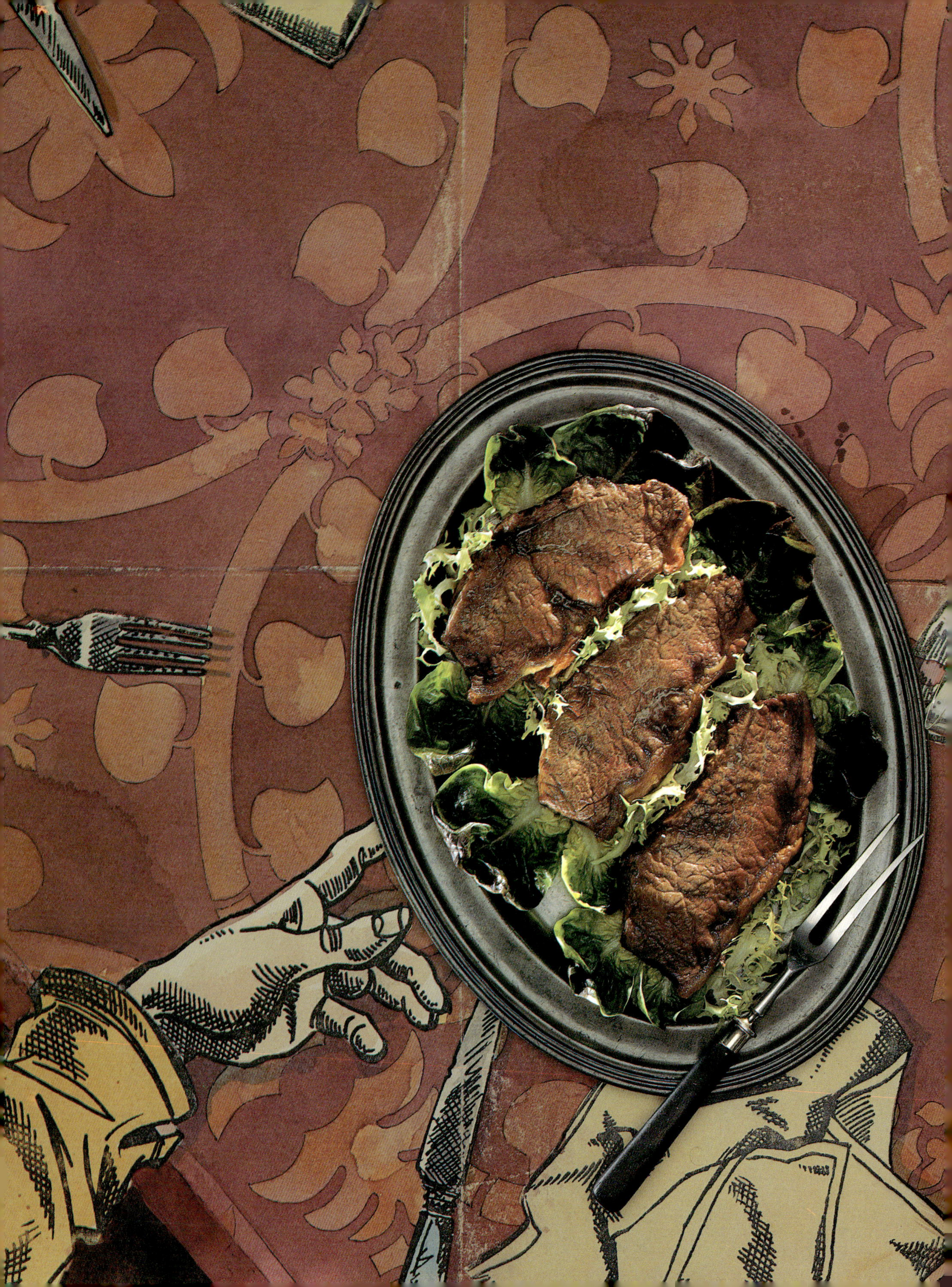

MEAT AND POULTRY 93

## GRILLED STEAK WITH GARLIC AND OLIVE OIL

### BISTECCA ALLA GRIGLIA CON AGLIO E OLIO

*The best way to enjoy these steaks, weather permitting, is to cook them on a barbecue with plenty of scented wood.*

**TIME 4–12 MINUTES, DEPENDING UPON HOW YOU LIKE YOUR STEAK!**

**4 sirloin steaks, each weighing about 175 g/6 oz, trimmed**
**3 garlic cloves, halved**
**4 tablespoons olive oil**
**salt and freshly milled black pepper**

**1** Heat the grill to high, or light the barbecue.

**2** Rub the steaks thoroughly all over with the garlic cloves.

**3** Brush the steaks generously with olive oil and grill to taste. When they are cooked, transfer them to a serving dish and sprinkle with salt and pepper and any leftover oil. Serve at once.

*Grilled steak with garlic and olive oil*

## THINLY SLICED FILLET OF BEEF WITH ROCKET
### FILETTO AFFETTATO CON LA RUCOLA

*I always eat this dish whenever I go to Milan and I find it a delightfully light way to enjoy beef. My favourite Italian restaurant in London also makes a dish very similar to this one, so now I do not have to travel quite so far! If you cannot find rocket, use two handfuls of big-leaved fresh basil.*

**TIME 15 MINUTES**

**12 very thin slices of beef fillet, about 500 g/1 lb, well trimmed**
**2 garlic cloves, very lightly crushed**
**3 tablespoons olive oil**
**salt and freshly milled black pepper**
**2 handfuls of rocket leaves, trimmed and rinsed**
**extra olive oil and balsamic vinegar, to serve**

**1** Rub the garlic all over the fillet.

**2** Drop the garlic into the olive oil and add 2 pinches of salt and plenty of pepper.

**3** Stir the mixture thoroughly, then lay the meat in the oil to marinate. Leave to stand for a few minutes while you heat the grill to high.

**4** Remove the meat from the mixture and arrange it in one layer on a metallic plate, or on foil, slightly overlapping.

**5** Put the meat under the very hot grill and seal it for 1 minute, then turn it over and seal it on the other side.

**6** Remove from the grill, arrange all the rocket on top of the meat to cover it completely and serve at once. Your guests might like to add oil, salt and pepper or balsamic vinegar to their portion.

## DUCK BREASTS WITH SICILIAN ORANGE SAUCE
### PETTI D'ANATRA CON SALSA D'ARANCE SICILIANE

*If you are lucky enough to find them, use the wonderful blood red oranges called* tarocchi *in their native Sicily. Otherwise, look for the juiciest blood oranges you can find.*

**TIME 15 MINUTES**

**2 tablespoons butter**
**4 duck breasts, each weighing about 175 g/6 oz, skinned and trimmed**
**2 tablespoons plain white flour**
**juice of 1 blood orange**
**1 blood orange, peeled and finely sliced**
**salt and freshly milled black pepper**
**1 blood orange, sliced, to garnish**
**parsley sprigs or orange leaves, to garnish**

**1** Melt the butter in a frying pan over a low heat.

**2** Coat the duck breasts in plain flour. Quickly seal the duck breasts in hot butter on both sides.

**3** Add the orange juice and cook gently over a low heat for about 3 minutes. Add the sliced orange and turn the breasts over. Cover and cook for a further 3 minutes.

**4** Uncover and season with salt and pepper, then arrange the duck breasts on a warmed serving platter. Garnish with the sliced orange and the parsley or orange leaves. Serve at once.

## TURKEY ESCALOPES WITH WHITE WINE AND HERBS

### SCALOPPINE DI TACCHINO CON VINO BIANCO ALLE ERBE MISTE

*The herbs listed below are not obligatory, just use whatever you have around, but make sure you use plenty! If you have only dried herbs, use only a quarter of the herb quantities.*

**TIME 20-25 MINUTES**

4 turkey escalopes, each weighing about 175 g/6 oz, trimmed
salt and freshly milled black pepper
1 tablespoon plain white flour
2-3 tablespoons olive oil
1 teaspoon chopped fresh rosemary
1 dessertspoon chopped fresh parsley
1 teaspoon chopped fresh tarragon
1 teaspoon chopped fresh sage
1 teaspoon chopped fresh marjoram
1 teaspoon chopped fresh thyme
½ teaspoon dried oregano
75 ml/2½ fl oz dry white wine

**1** Flatten the turkey escalopes with a meat mallet; if they are very large, cut them in half.

**2** Season the flour and toss the escalopes in the flour just enough to coat them, shaking off any excess flour.

**3** Heat the oil in a large frying pan with the herbs until the oil is sizzling. Quickly seal the floured meat in the pan on both sides. Cook the meat for 6-8 minutes on each side until golden brown.

**4** Arrange the meat on a warmed serving platter.

**5** Add the wine to the pan and stir thoroughly, scraping the bottom of the pan to loosen any flour that has stuck there. Pour the resulting sauce over the meat and serve at once with a fresh salad and some crusty bread.

## DUCK BREASTS WITH PINE KERNELS

### PETTI D'ANATRA CON I PINOLI

**TIME 25-30 MINUTES**

4 duck breasts, each weighing about 175 g/6 oz, skins removed
2 tablespoons olive oil
1 garlic clove, chopped
3 tablespoons pine kernels
1 small sprig fresh rosemary
grated rind of 1 orange
salt and freshly milled black pepper
3 tablespoons dry red wine
juice of 1 large orange
1 large teaspoon runny honey
1 orange, sliced, to garnish

**1** Heat the grill. Trim and flatten the duck breasts. if necessary cut them in half. Grill the duck breasts just enough to seal them on either side for about 3 minutes. This will also get rid of some of the fat, which can be discarded or saved for another recipe.

**2** Meanwhile, heat the oil slowly with the garlic, pine kernels, rosemary and orange rind. Stir and simmer this mixture for about 5 minutes, then place the duck breasts in the pan. Season with salt and pepper. Continue cooking them over a very low heat for about 10-12 minutes, basting and turning them frequently.

**3** Pour over the wine and boil quickly to evaporate the alcohol, then remove the breasts from the pan and arrange them on a warmed dish. Keep hot.

**4** Pour the orange juice into the pan and stir all the ingredients together. Boil to reduce slightly.

**5** Stir in the honey until melted, then pour the sauce over the duck breasts. Garnish with the slices of orange and serve at once.

**OVERLEAF**
*Duck breasts with Sicilian orange sauce*

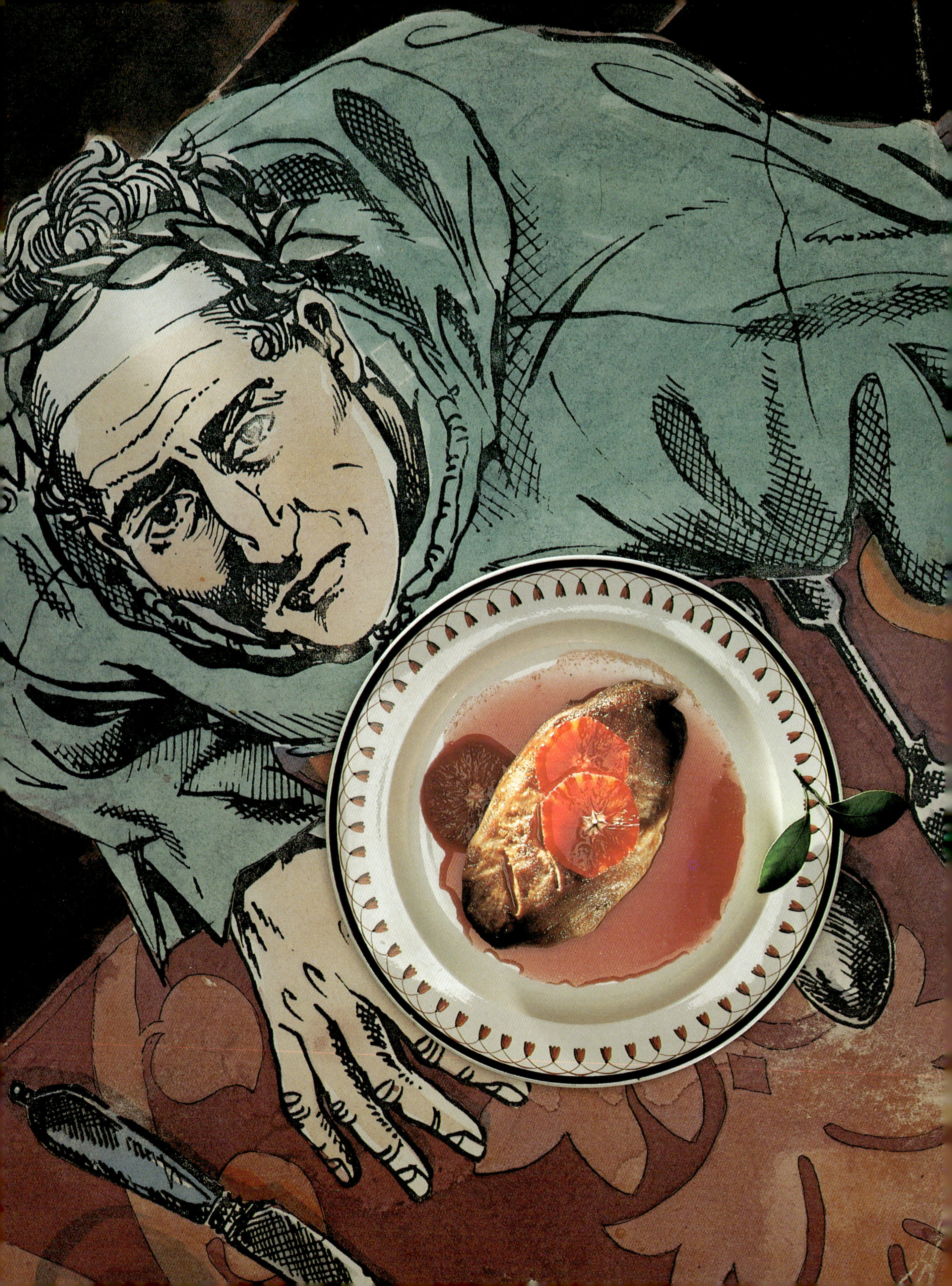

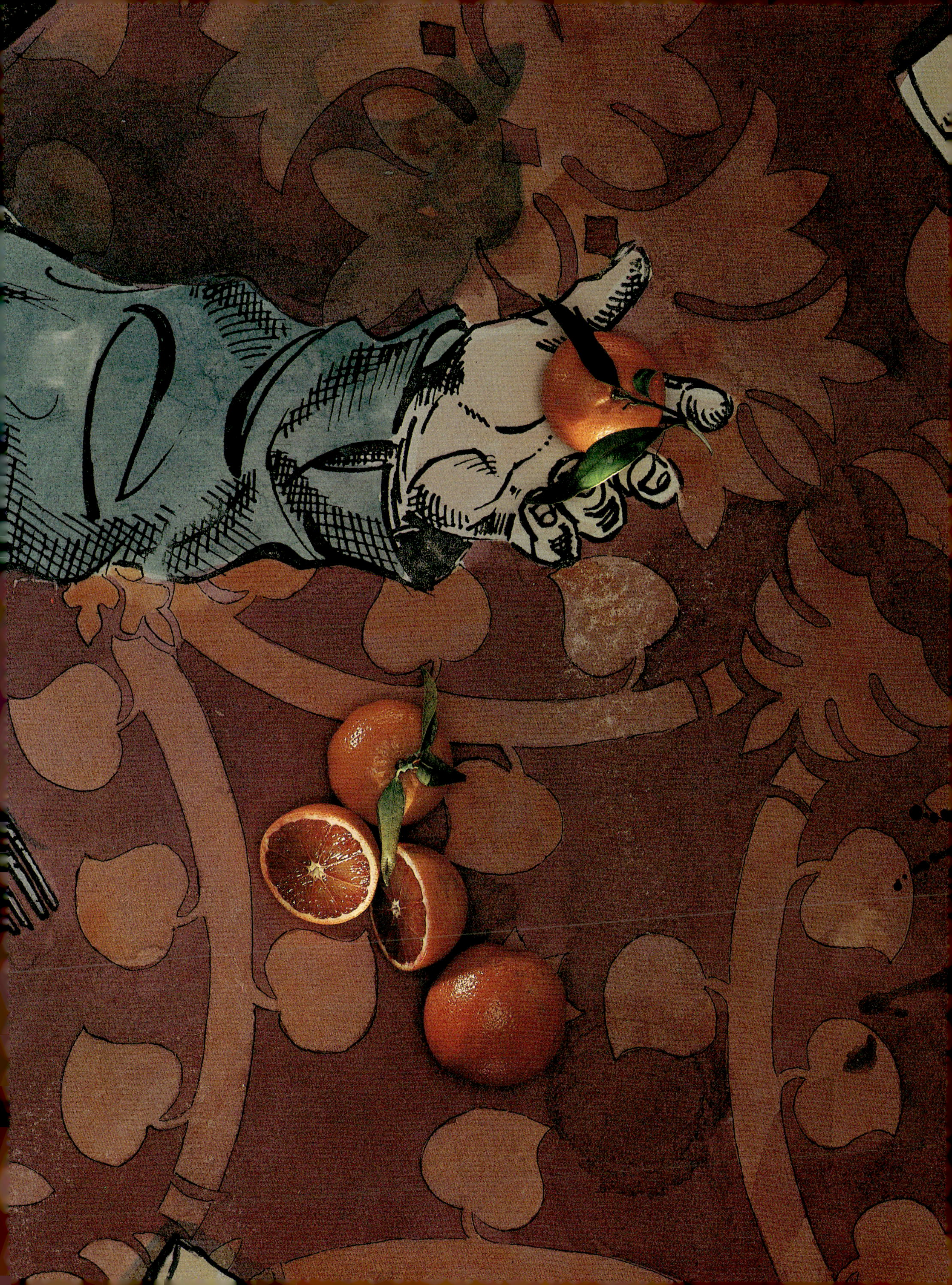

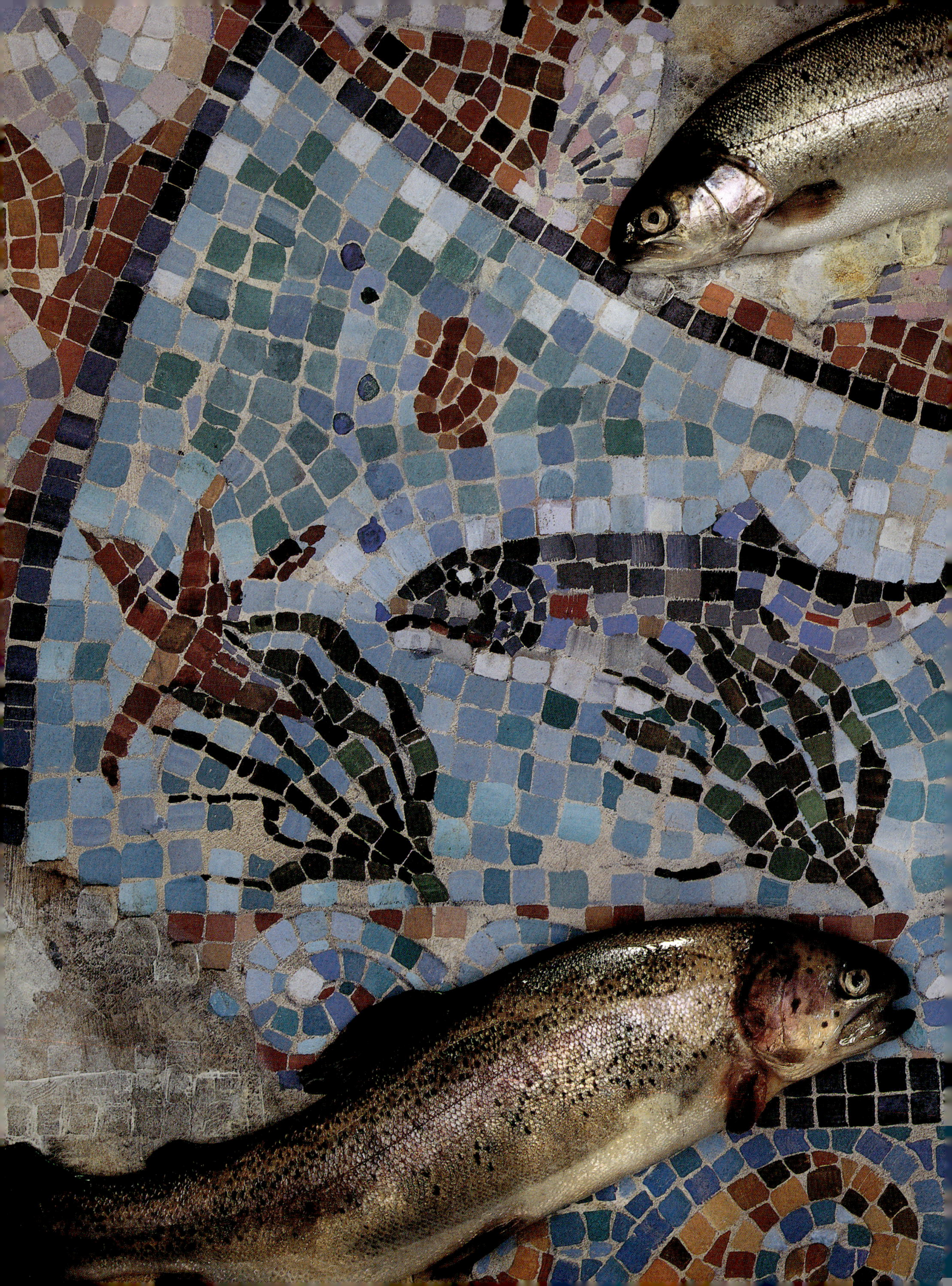

# FISH
*and*
SHELLFISH

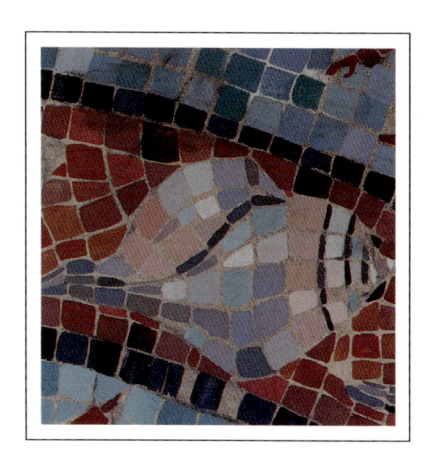

*Fish and shellfish have always featured prominently in the Italian diet, because they are low in fat and high in protein, and are ideally suited to quick cooking.*

## MUSSELS IN SAFFRON MAYONNAISE
### COZZE IN UNA MAIONESE ALLO ZAFFERANO

*A lovely summertime dish of cool mussels. As an alternative, mix two cloves of crushed garlic into the mayonnaise instead of the saffron.*

**TIME 20 MINUTES**

40 fresh, live mussels, very carefully scrubbed and rinsed thoroughly
3 sprigs fresh parsley
½ lemon
2 tablespoons dry white wine
5 tablespoons ready-made mayonnaise
2 tablespoons thick, natural yoghurt
1 sachet powdered saffron, approximately 3 g
salt and freshly milled black pepper
3 tablespoons chopped fresh parsley

**1** Discard any open mussels. Put all the cleaned mussels into a large pan with the parsley sprigs, halved lemon and wine. Cover and shake the pan gently over a medium heat until all the mussels open. This should take about 6 minutes.

**2** Remove the pan from the heat and take all the mussels out of their shells, discarding all the unopened ones. Keep a few shells for the garnish, and discard the rest.

**3** Strain the liquid in the bottom of the pan through muslin and set aside.

**4** Arrange the shelled mussels in a dish.

**5** Beat the mayonnaise and the yoghurt together with the saffron, salt and pepper and parsley. Add just enough of the cooking liquid to make a smooth sauce. Pour the sauce all over the mussels.

**6** Garnish the edges of the dish with the shells and serve at once.

## SQUID WITH GARLIC AND OLIVE OIL
### SEPPIE CON AGLIO E OLIO

**TIME 20 MINUTES**

4 large squid or 8 smaller ones, cleaned and gutted
7 tablespoons extra-virgin olive oil
4 garlic cloves, crushed to a paste
salt and freshly milled black pepper
3 tablespoons fresh chopped parsley

**1** Put the squid in a plastic bag and use a meat mallet or the side of a heavy knife to beat them gently through the plastic in order to tenderize them as much as possible.

**2** Meanwhile, heat the grill to medium.

**3** Put the olive oil, garlic, salt and pepper and about two-thirds of the parsley in a jam jar and screw the top on tightly. Shake the jar very hard to make a smooth amalgamation.

**4** Take the squid out of the bag and slice them lengthways into several pieces each. Put them in a bowl, pour over the garlic dressing and mix them together with your hands, then arrange the squid strips on the grill.

**5** Grill for about 7 minutes, turning the pieces of squid frequently and sprinkling generously with the remaining oil. Transfer to a warmed serving dish and sprinkle with the rest of the parsley. Serve immediately.

## TROUT WITH CHILLI AND OLIVE OIL
### TROTA CON PEPERONCINO E OLIO D'OLIVA

*This is a very simple way to spice up an otherwise fairly bland fish. If you want a punchy flavour against a creamy texture, then this is a dish for you. As this is really quite fiery, reduce the amount of chilli according to taste.*

**TIME 20 MINUTES**

**4 whole trout, each weighing about 250 g/8 oz, gutted and washed carefully**
**2 dried red chilli peppers, rubbed lightly in your palms and cut in half**
**10 tablespoons olive oil**
**4 small sprigs fresh rosemary, chopped**
**3 garlic cloves, crushed to a paste**
**salt and freshly milled black pepper**

**1** Heat the grill to medium.

**2** Meanwhile, slash the fish 4 times on each side across the skin to the backbone. Slice some of the chilli and put a generous piece inside each fish.

**3** Chop the remaining chilli very finely and mix it thoroughly with the olive oil, rosemary and garlic and season. Spread this mixture all over both sides of the fish and inside each fish, reserving just enough to sprinkle over the fish at the end.

**4** Grill for about 7 minutes on each side depending upon the thickness of the fish, until cooked through: you can tell when it is cooked because the eyes become white and the point of a knife inserted through the thickest part of the fish slides in easily. Transfer to a warm dish and sprinkle with the reserved oil before serving.

## MUSSELS WITH GARLIC AND CORIANDER
### COZZE ALL'AGLIO CON IL CORIANDOLO FRESCO

**TIME 15 MINUTES**

**40-50 fresh live mussels, well scrubbed**
**1 wine glass dry white wine**
**1 lemon, halved**
**1 large handful of fresh coriander**
**2-3 garlic cloves, halved**
**salt and freshly milled black pepper**
**1 ciabatta loaf, or other coarse Italian bread, sliced thinly**
**3 tablespoons thick, natural yoghurt**

**1** Discard any opened mussels. Put the mussels into a large pan with the wine, the lemon, half the coriander and the halved garlic. Season with salt and pepper, cover and shake the pan over a medium heat until all the mussels are open. This should take about 6 minutes.

**2** Remove the pan from the heat and remove the mussels from the pan. Discard any shells that have not opened.

**3** Heat the grill to high, and toast the bread slices very gently on either side.

**4** Strain the cooking liquid and return it to the pan. Add the yoghurt, chop the remaining coriander and stir into the liquid. Return the mussels to the saucepan and stir. As soon as they are heated through, remove from the heat.

**5** Place the toasts on a serving dish, or in individual soup plates. Pour over all the mussels and all their liquid. Serve immediately.

**OVERLEAF**
**Left** *Trout with chilli and olive oil*
**Right** *Mussels with garlic and coriander*

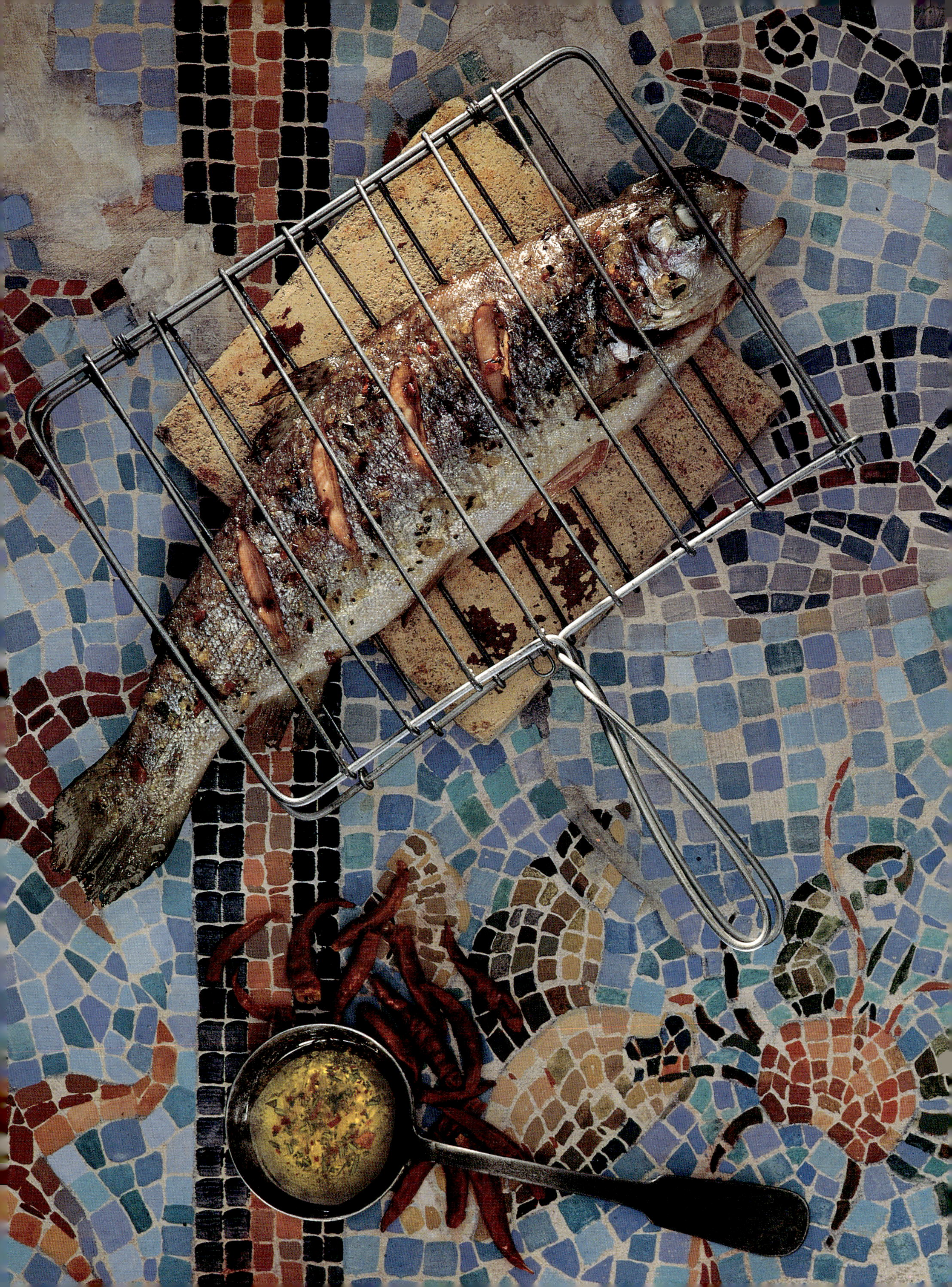

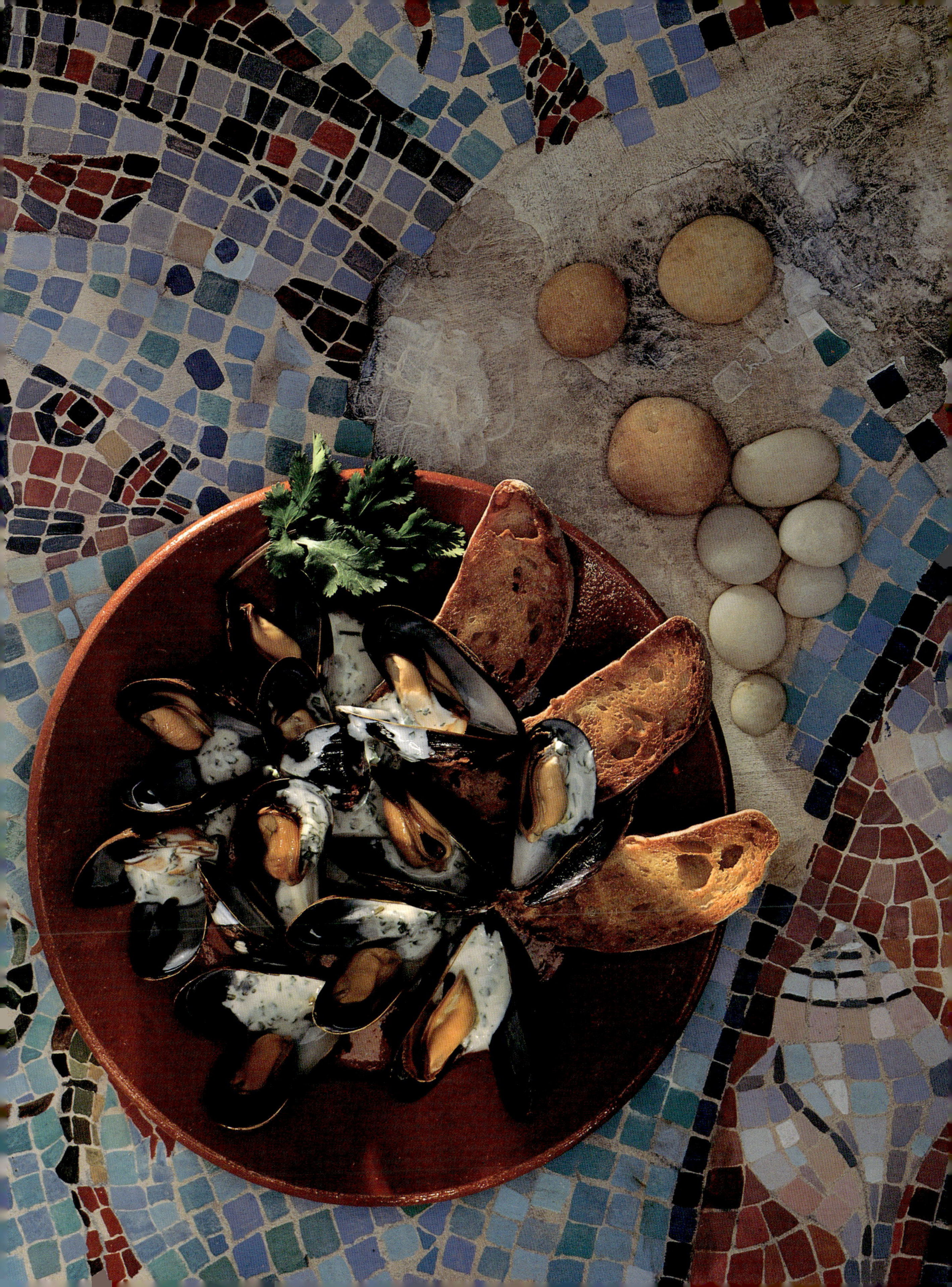

## CLAMS WITH CHILLI ON TOASTED CIABATTA

### VONGOLE AL PEPERONCINO SULLA CIABATTA

*Clams can be very gritty and muddy, so be sure you wash them very thoroughly. Look for the tiny clams from Italy called vongole. These are also available canned or preserved in brine in glass jars.*

**TIME 15 MINUTES**

1 kg/2 lb fresh live clams, well rinsed
4 tablespoons olive oil
2 garlic cloves, finely chopped
2 dried red chilli peppers, finely chopped
salt and freshly milled black pepper
3 tablespoons chopped fresh parsley
8 slices ciabatta bread, or other coarse Italian bread, toasted

**1** Discard any opened clams. Place the clams in a pan over a medium heat, covered, for about 5 minutes, to open. Remove the pan from the heat and take all the molluscs out of their shells. Discard any clams that have not opened.

**2** Strain the cooking liquid through muslin.

**3** Heat the oil in a large frying pan with the garlic and chilli over low heat until soft. Add the shelled clams and stir through to heat thoroughly. Add a little salt and pepper and the cooking liquid. Stir in the parsley and take off the heat.

**4** Place the toasted bread on a serving dish or on individual plates. Cover each slice of bread with an even amounts of clams. Serve at once.

## FILLETS OF SOLE WITH OYSTER MUSHROOMS

### FILETTI DI SOGLIOLA CON I FUNGHI

*The delicate combination of flavours and textures of this dish make it fairly sophisticated. It is also not particularly cheap, so it's a good dish for a simple dinner party when you haven't got much time, but the food needs to be impressive.*

**TIME 15 MINUTES**

14 oyster mushrooms
4 large lemon soles, each weighing about 300 g/9 oz, filleted
3 tablespoons butter
2 teaspoons lemon juice
3 tablespoons dry white wine
salt and freshly milled black pepper
3 tablespoons chopped parsley, to garnish

**1** Clean and thickly slice 10 mushrooms, keeping 4 whole ones for the garnish.

**2** Melt the butter in a large frying pan, toss in the mushrooms with the lemon juice and mix together. Cook gently for about 5 minutes, until just softened, then lay the fish on top.

**3** Shake the pan and spoon mushrooms and butter over the fish to baste. Pour on the wine and allow the alcohol to boil off for 1-2 minutes.

**4** Turn the fish over after 3 minutes and cook for a further 2 minutes on the other side. Sprinkle with a little salt and pepper and arrange on a warmed serving dish. Arrange the mushrooms over and around the fish, garnish with the chopped parsley and the 4 whole mushrooms, and serve at once.

*Fillets of sole with oyster mushrooms*

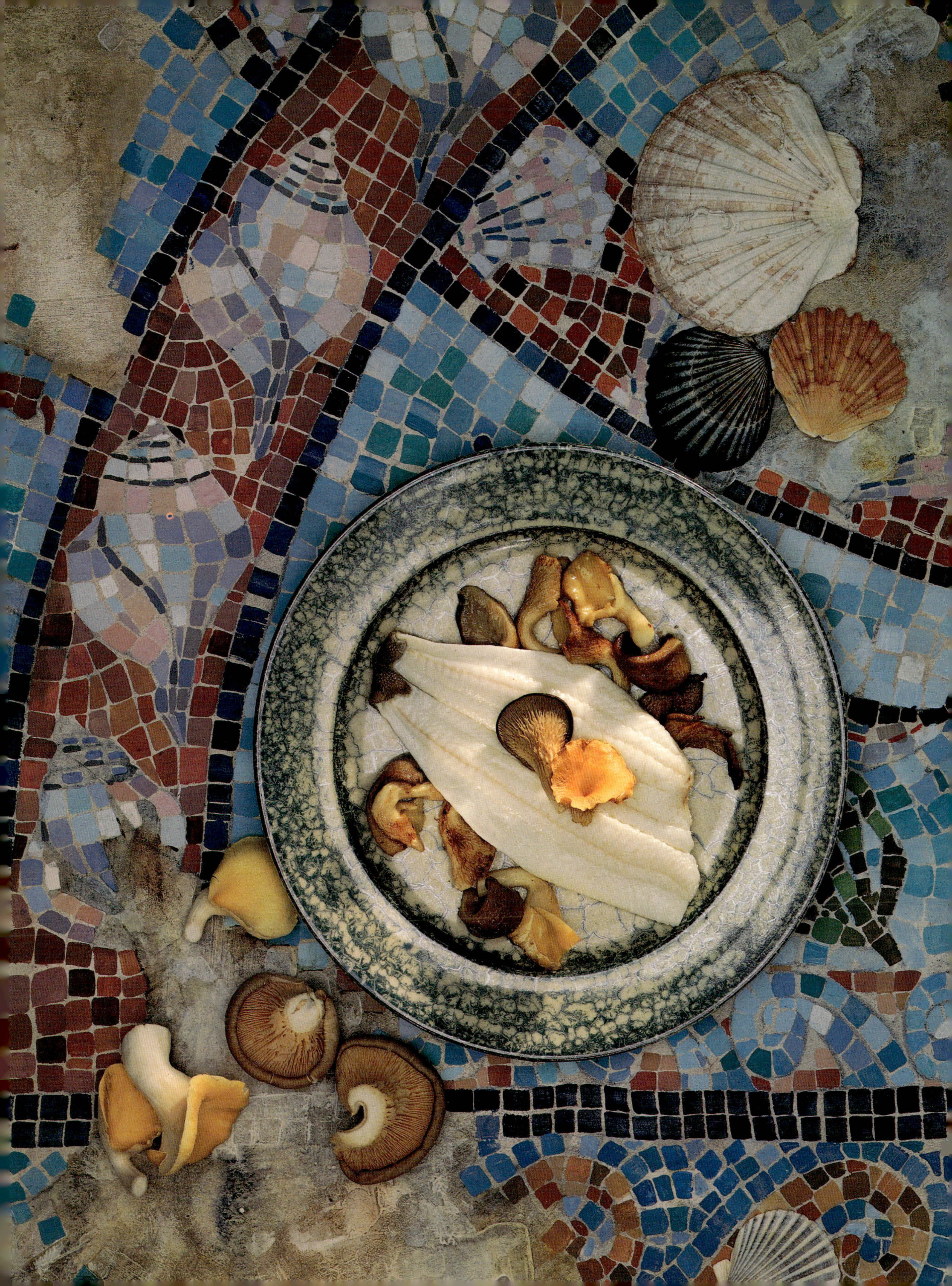

## MINI SALMON STEAKS POACHED IN PROSECCO

### SALMONE LESSATO NEL PROSECCO

*Another simple dinner party recipe, perfect for really special occasions.*

**TIME 20 MINUTES**

½ bottle Prosecco or other dry sparkling wine
8 very small salmon steaks, each weighing about 75 g/3 oz, well trimmed if necessary
salt
1 small sprig rosemary, very finely chopped
½ lemon, thinly sliced
4-5 tablespoons double cream or thick, natural yoghurt

**1** Pour the wine into a wide, deep frying pan with a lid. Lay the fish in the wine and bring to a very gentle boil, then simmer for about 3-4 minutes, uncovered, on both sides, depending upon how thick the steaks are.

**2** Sprinkle the rosemary all over the fish.

**3** Lay the sliced lemon on top of the cooked fish and turn off the heat. Cover and leave to stand for 3 minutes. Transfer on to a warmed serving dish.

**4** Strain the cooking liquor into a bowl to remove any skin or scales. Return the strained liquor to a clean pan and boil rapidly to reduce by half.

**5** Stir the cream or yoghurt into the strained liquor, season to taste and pour over the fish.

## PAN-FRIED PLAICE WITH PEAS AND CREAM

### PLATESSA CON I PISELLI E LA PANNA

**TIME 15 MINUTES**

8 small unskinned plaice fillets, each weighing about 50 g/2 oz, folded in half lengthways
2 tablespoons plain white flour
3 tablespoons butter
5 tablespoons dry vermouth
6 tablespoons frozen petits pois
salt and freshly milled black pepper
5 tablespoons double cream

**1** Coat each folded fillet lightly in the flour, shaking off any excess.

**2** Heat the butter until foaming in a large pan. Lay the fish in the butter and seal on both sides of the folded fillet for about 20 seconds.

**3** Pour over the vermouth and boil off the alcohol for 1 minute. Add the peas and season with salt and pepper. Spoon the butter and peas over the fish fillets.

**4** Cover and continue to cook for about 3 minutes, until the fish flakes easily when tested with the tip of a knife.

**5** Take the fish out of the pan and keep warm on a dish. Pour in the cream and raise the heat to bring the cream just to the boil, stirring constantly. Pour the sauce over the fish and serve at once.

## DEEP-FRIED PRAWNS AND SQUID RINGS WITH LEMON SAUCE

### FRITTO DI GAMBERI E SEPPIE AL LIMONE

*A very easy and light version of the classic* fritto misto. *You can also use this batter for frying strips of courgette, cubes of mozzarella and even fresh artichoke hearts.*

**TIME 20 MINUTES**

8 large cooked prawns, heads and shells on
8 thin squid rings with a wide diameter
2 egg yolks
4 tablespoons self-raising flour
250 ml/8 fl oz milk
2 egg whites, whisked until stiff
juice of 1 lemon, strained
3 tablespoons olive oil
1 tablespoon chopped fresh parsley
grated rind of ½ lemon
salt and freshly milled black pepper
sunflower oil for deep-frying

**1** Wash and dry the prawns and squid carefully.

**2** Beat the egg yolks with a balloon whisk until pale yellow. Blend in the flour, then mix in the milk. Whisk thoroughly to remove all the lumps. Fold in the egg whites. Put the batter in the fridge for a few minutes while you prepare the sauce.

**3** Blend the lemon juice and the oil together. Stir in the parsley and the lemon rind. Season with salt and pepper and set aside until required. Stir again just before serving.

**4** Heat the oil until a small piece of bread dropped into the oil sizzles instantly. Dip the prawns and squid into the batter to coat them completely and then fry them for about 5 minutes or until crispy and golden brown. Cook in 2 batches if necessary.

**5** Drain the fried prawns and squid on kitchen paper and then arrange on a serving plate. Serve immediately, with the lemon sauce to dip into, remembering to remove the heads and tails of the prawns before eating!

## GRILLED SALMON WITH PESTO

### CODE DI SALMONE ALLA GRIGLIA COL PESTO

*This is a very easy way to serve fresh salmon, which is widely available in neat tail fillets. Of course, if you make the dish using home-made pesto, it will taste even better.*

**TIME 30 MINUTES**

5 tablespoons good-quality pesto
5 tablespoons dry white wine
4 salmon tail fillets or steaks, each weighing about 175 g/6 oz
freshly milled black pepper
fresh basil leaves, to garnish

**1** Mix the pesto with the wine. Put the salmon in a deep dish and pour the diluted pesto over it. Leave to stand for about 15 minutes, turning the fish frequently. Meanwhile, heat the grill to medium.

**2** Grill the fish for about 3-5 minutes on each side, basting frequently with the pesto, until the flesh flakes easily when tested with the tip of a knife.

**3** Pour the remaining pesto over and heat through at maximum heat for about 1 minute. Remove from the heat, sprinkle with a little freshly milled black pepper, garnish with the fresh basil and serve immediately.

**OVERLEAF**
**Left** *Deep-fried prawns and squid rings with lemon sauce*
**Right** *Grilled salmon with pesto*

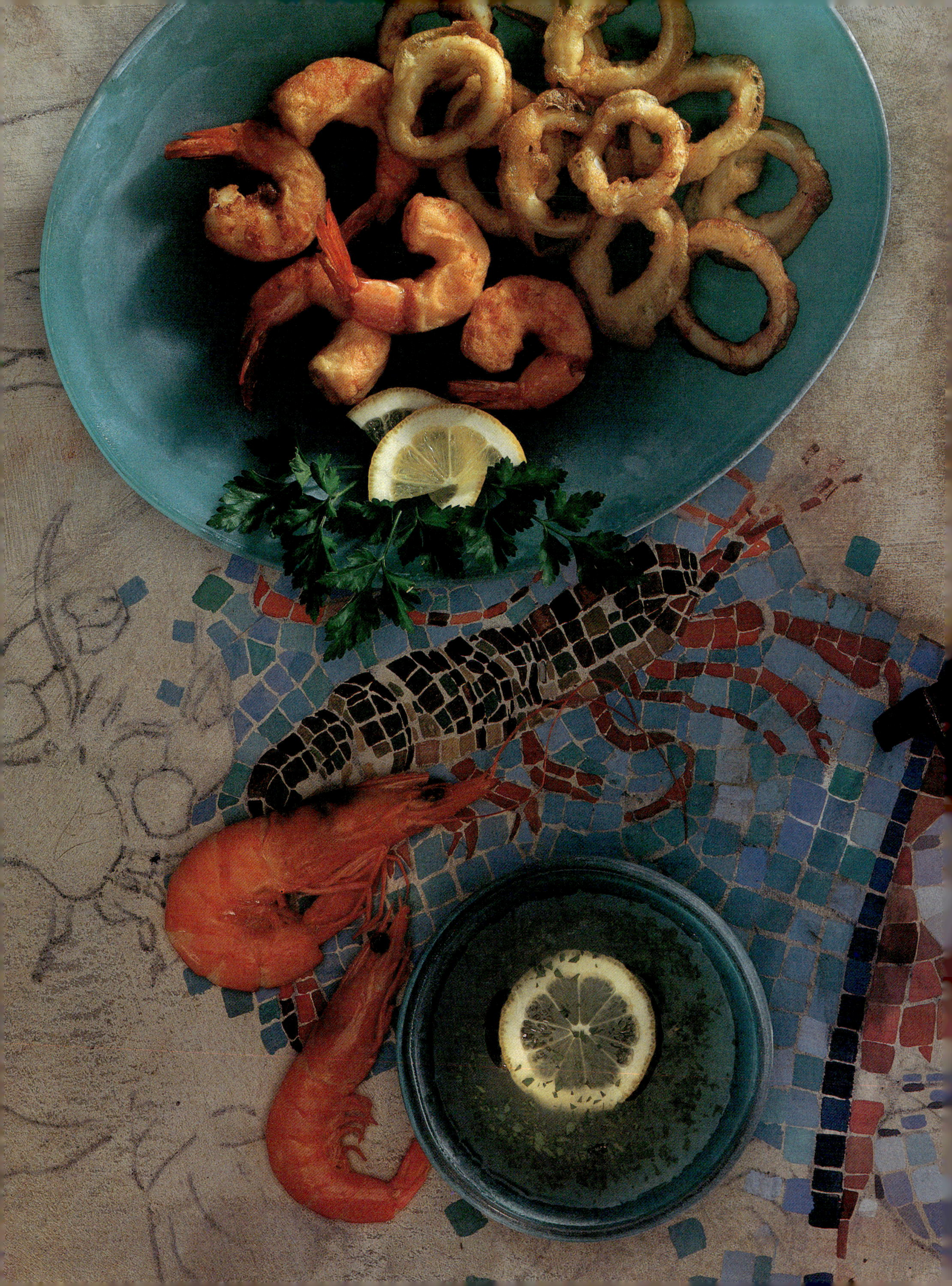

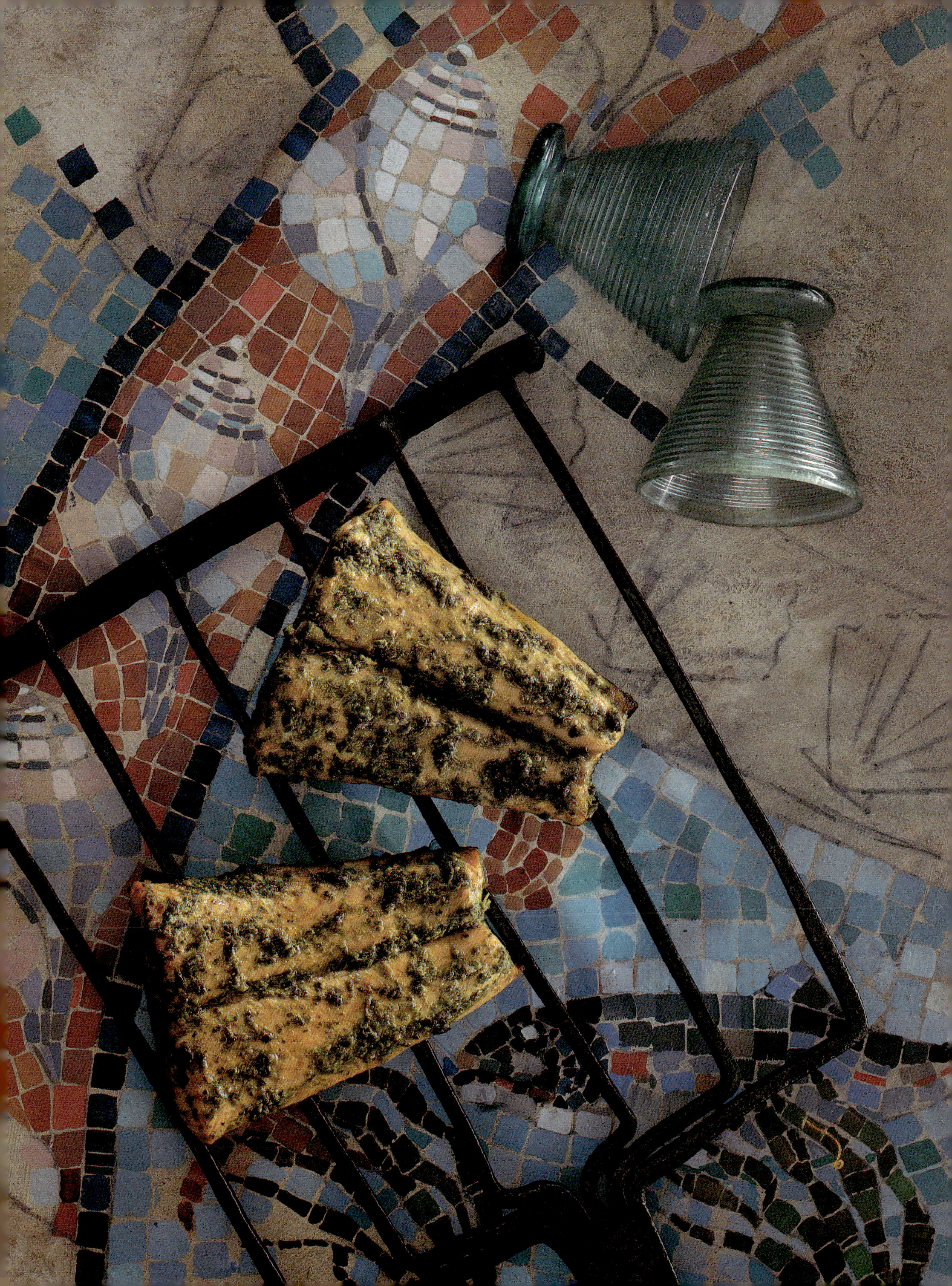

## GRILLED SWORDFISH STEAKS WITH OLIVE OIL AND LEMON

### PESCE SPADA ALLA GRIGLIA CON OLIO D'OLIVA E LIMONE

*Eating this is guaranteed to make you feel like you have just arrived in Sicily!*

**TIME 20 MINUTES**

**4 large swordfish or shark or fresh tuna steaks, about 200 g/7 oz each**
**juice of 1 lemon**
**1 teaspoon grated lemon rind**
**5 tablespoons olive oil**
**1 teaspoon dried oregano**
**salt and freshly milled black pepper**
**lemon wedges, to garnish**

**1** Heat the grill to high.

**2** Lay the fish in a dish and beat together the lemon juice, lemon rind, olive oil and oregano until thickened and cloudy. Stir in salt and pepper and pour this all over the fish. Turn the fish over to coat thoroughly.

**3** Grill the fish for about 5 minutes on either side, basting constantly with the remaining sauce, until the fish flakes easily when tested with a fork. Serve at once, garnished with lemon wedges.

*Grilled swordfish steaks with olive oil and lemon*

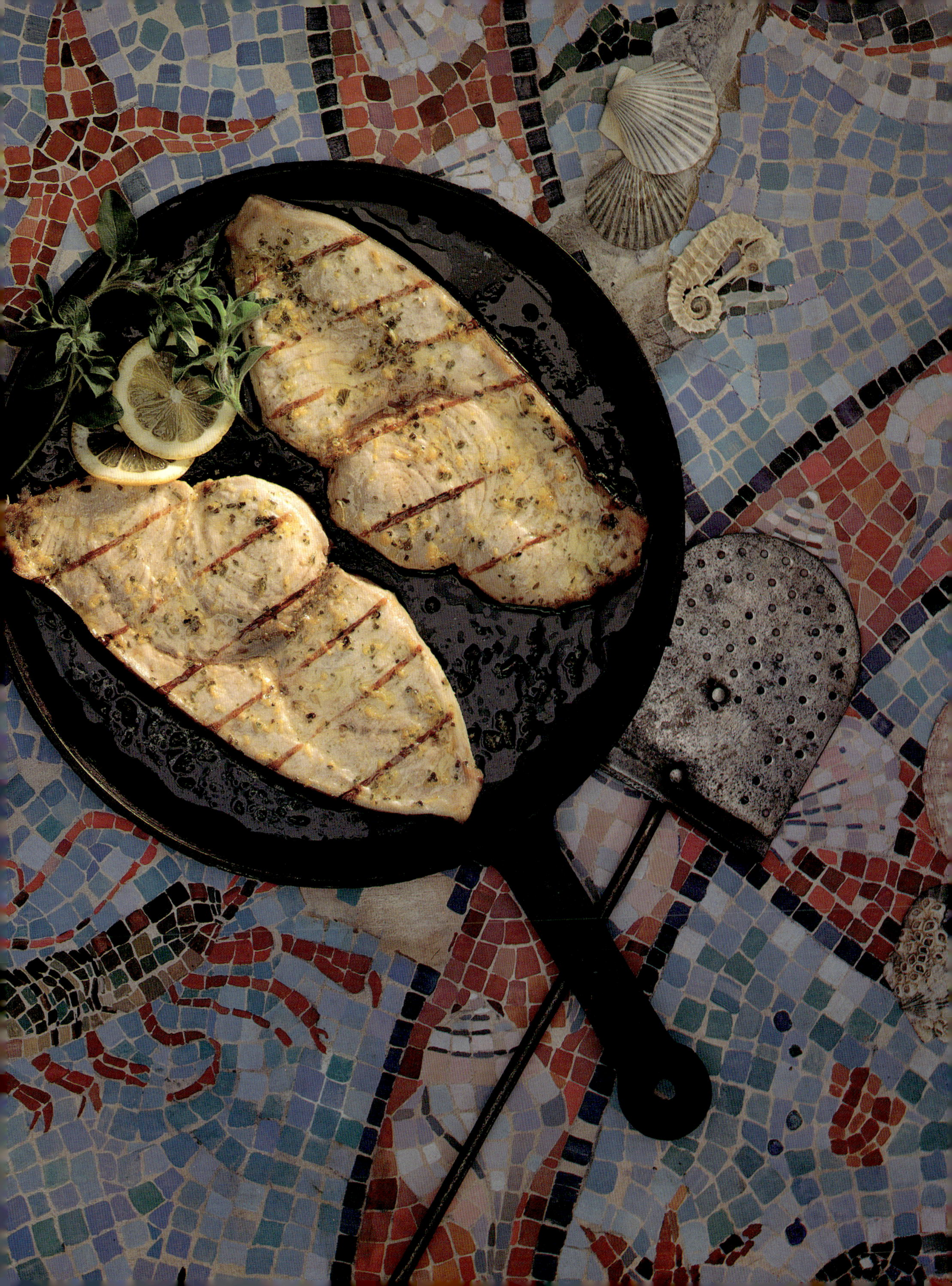

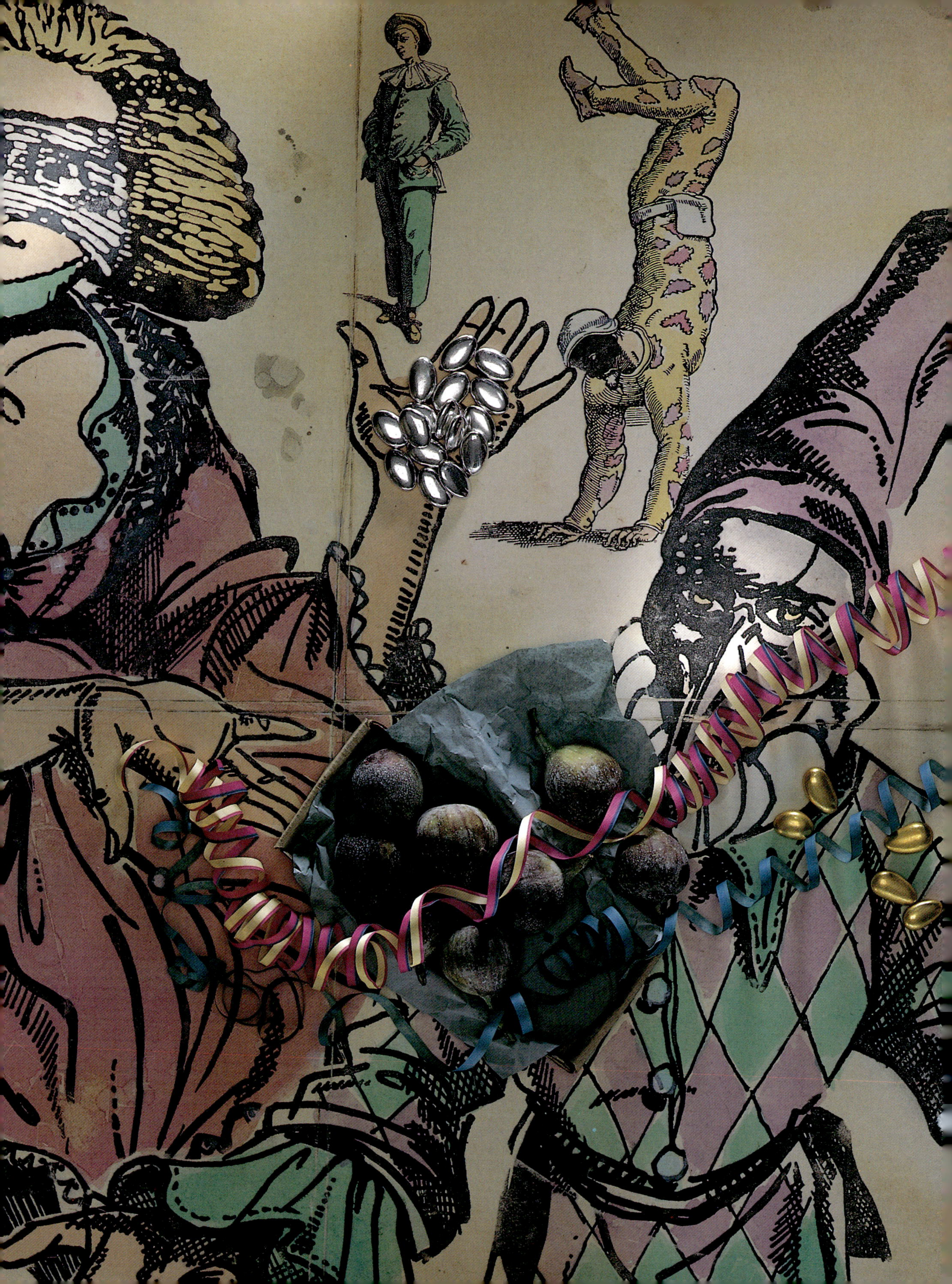

# FRUIT
*and*
# DESSERTS

*In Italy, the trees and market stalls are always heavy with luscious and plentiful fruit. It is, quite simply, the quickest and healthiest way to end a meal.*

## ICE CREAM DROWNED IN ESPRESSO
### AFFOGATO AL CAFFÈ

*There are lots of different kinds of* affogato *made by adding either a liqueur or coffee to good-quality vanilla ice cream (not 'soft-scoop').*

**TIME 5 MINUTES**

8 scoops dairy vanilla ice cream
4 tiny espresso cups of espresso coffee, unsweetened
*langues de chat* **biscuits, to serve**

**1** Put 2 scoops of ice cream into each of 4 sundae glasses or pretty glass bowls.

**2** Pour 1 cup of boiling hot espresso over each serving of ice cream.

**3** Serve immediately with the *langues de chat*.

## HOT APPLE AND AMARETTO CUPS
### COPPE CALDE DI MELE E AMARETTI

*A very simple, delicious dish. A scoop of vanilla ice cream improves it even more! If you store the cups in a cool place for an hour or so, the biscuits have time to soften and take on the taste of the liqueur.*

**TIME 20 MINUTES**

4 Bramley apples, peeled, cored and cubed
2 tablespoons cold water
2 tablespoons sugar
12 amaretti biscuits
5 tablespoons Amaretto liqueur

**1** Put the apples into a saucepan with the sugar and water and cook for about 10 minutes without the lid until the apples turn mushy and fluffy.

**2** Meanwhile, put all the biscuits into a plastic bag and crush with a rolling pin to make a coarse crumb mixture.

**3** Remove the soft apples from the heat. Arrange the biscuit crumbs and the cooked apples into sundae type glasses in layers, sprinkling each layer of biscuits with Amaretto liqueur. Finish off each glass with a layer of apple. Serve at once, or chill until required.

## FRESH FIGS WITH MARASCHINO AND CREAM

### FICHI FRESCHI CON LA PANNA E IL MARASCHINO

*It is hard to imagine improving upon fresh figs, they are so incredibly delicious as they are, superb with prosciutto and fantastic with salame. However, the flavours of maraschino and brown sugar, added to the luxury of cream, make a very special dessert out of this wonderful fruit.*

**TIME 10 MINUTES**

**12 fresh figs**
**5 tablespoons maraschino**
**3 tablespoons flaked almonds**
**6 tablespoons extra-thick double cream**
**2 tablespoons single cream**
**2 teaspoons soft brown sugar**

**1** Peel the figs very carefully so as not to break them up. Cut them in half and arrange them in a single layer in a shallow glass dish.

**2** Pour the maraschino all over the figs. Cover with the almonds.

**3** Mix the creams together very thoroughly, then cover the figs and almonds with the cream without disrupting the layers.

**4** Sprinkle with the soft brown sugar and chill until required.

## HOT PEARS WITH CREAMY GORGONZOLA

### PERE CALDE AL GORGONZOLA

**TIME 20 MINUTES**

**4 large pears, peeled and quartered**
**2 glasses dry white wine**
**3 tablespoons caster sugar**
**100 g/4 oz Gorgonzola cheese, sliced into 8 strips**

**1** Put the pears into a saucepan and cover with the wine. Sprinkle the sugar over the pears and poach uncovered until just tender, for about 5 minutes.

**2** Take the pears out of the saucepan and arrange in a flameproof dish. Surround with the cooking juices. Heat the grill.

**3** Insert a slice or two of cheese between each pear quarter. Place under the grill until the cheese runs. Serve at once.

**OVERLEAF**
**Left** *Fresh figs with maraschino and cream*
**Right** *Hot pears with creamy Gorgonzola*

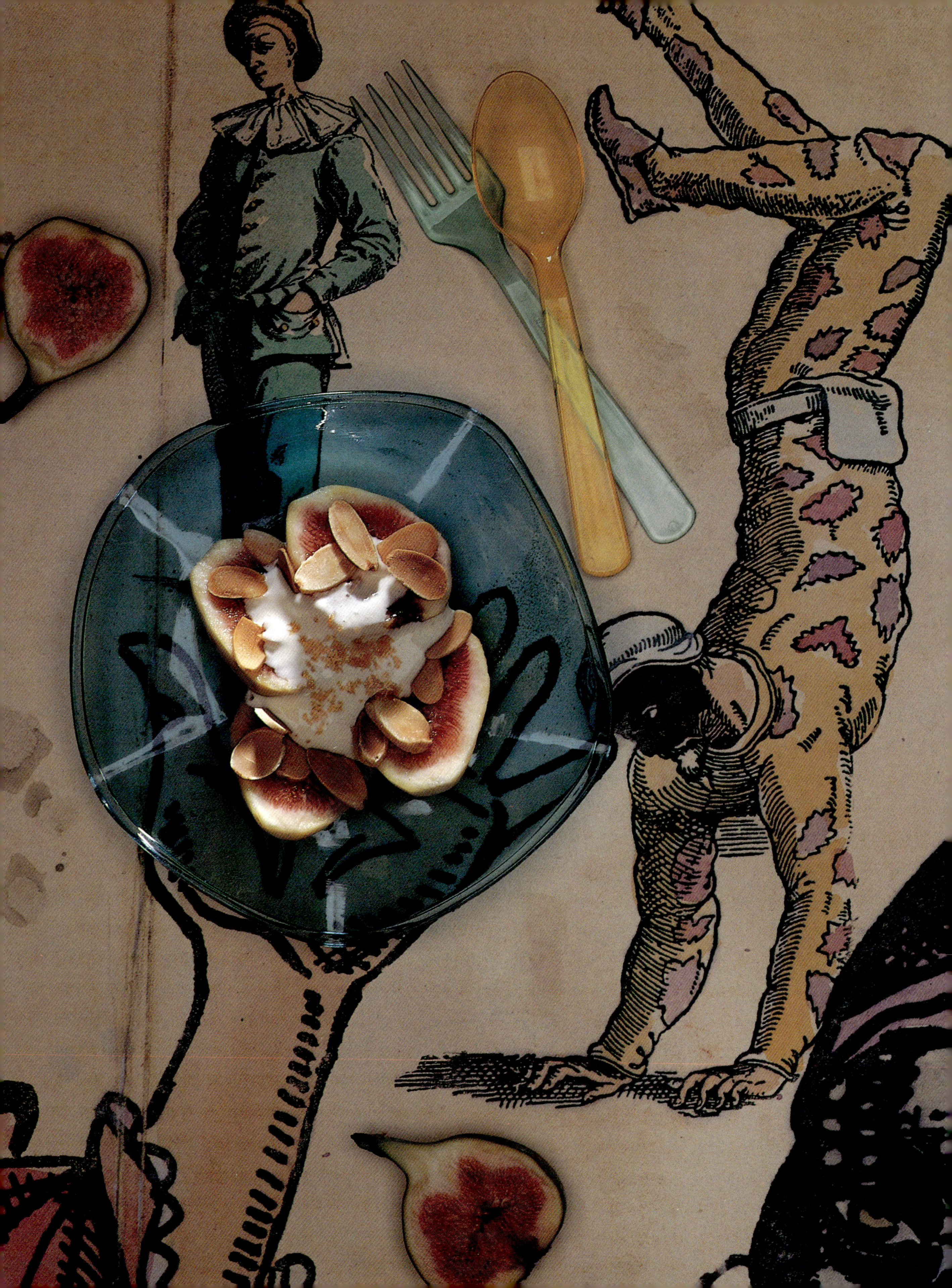

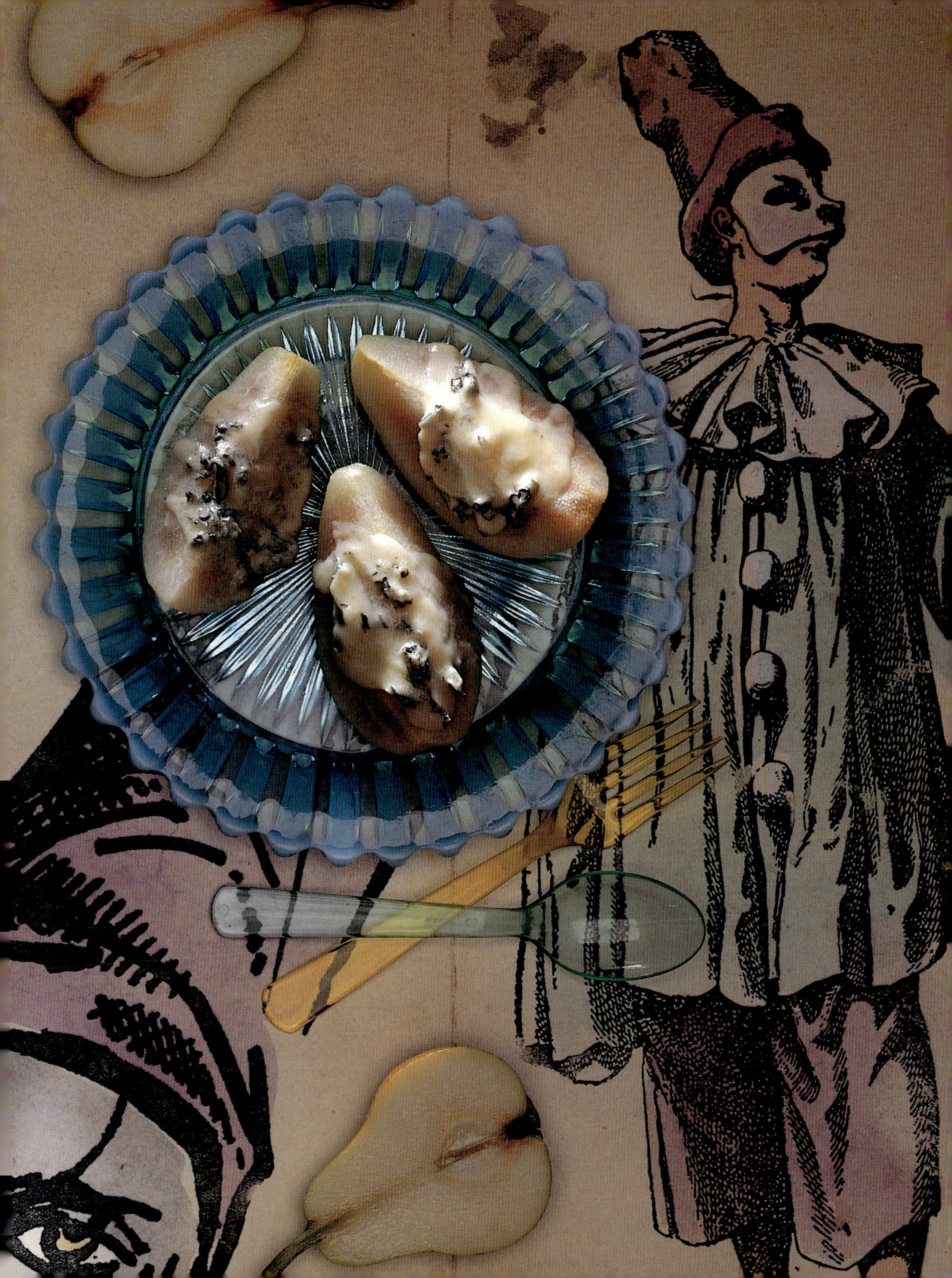

## ICE CREAM DROWNED IN BRANDY
### AFFOGATO AL BRANDY

*I like to use Vecchia Romagna, the best known brand of Italian brandy, but you will enjoy this quick end to a meal with whatever brandy you have to hand. Don't forget to transfer the ice cream from the freezer to the refrigerator about 15 minutes before you are ready to serve so it will be soft enough to scoop.*

**TIME 3 MINUTES**

**8 scoops dairy vanilla ice cream**
**4-8 tablespoons brandy**
**8 sponge fingers or almond biscuits**

**1** Put 2 scoops of ice cream into each of 4 sundae glasses or pretty glass bowls.

**2** Pour 1-2 tablespoons brandy on top of each portion. Serve immediately with the biscuits.

## HOT BLACKBERRY FRITTERS
### FRITTELLE DI MORE

**TIME 25 MINUTES**

**250 g/8 oz day-old white bread, crusts removed**
**200 ml/7 fl oz milk**
**sunflower oil for deep-frying**
**120 g/4½ oz plain white flour**
**3 eggs, beaten**
**200 g/7 oz blackberries**
**caster sugar for dusting**

**1** Soak the bread in the milk, then squeeze it a little in your hands.

**2** Heat the oil in a deep saucepan or deep-fat fryer, until it sizzles and a cube of bread dropped into it browns instantly.

**3** Meanwhile, mix the flour, eggs and berries into the saturated bread. Add a little more milk if it appears to be a bit too stiff.

**4** When the oil is sizzling hot, slide spoonfuls of the batter into the oil using 2 large spoons. Fry until puffed and crispy, then scoop out of the oil and drain on kitchen paper. Dust with plenty of caster sugar and serve hot.

*Hot blackberry fritters*

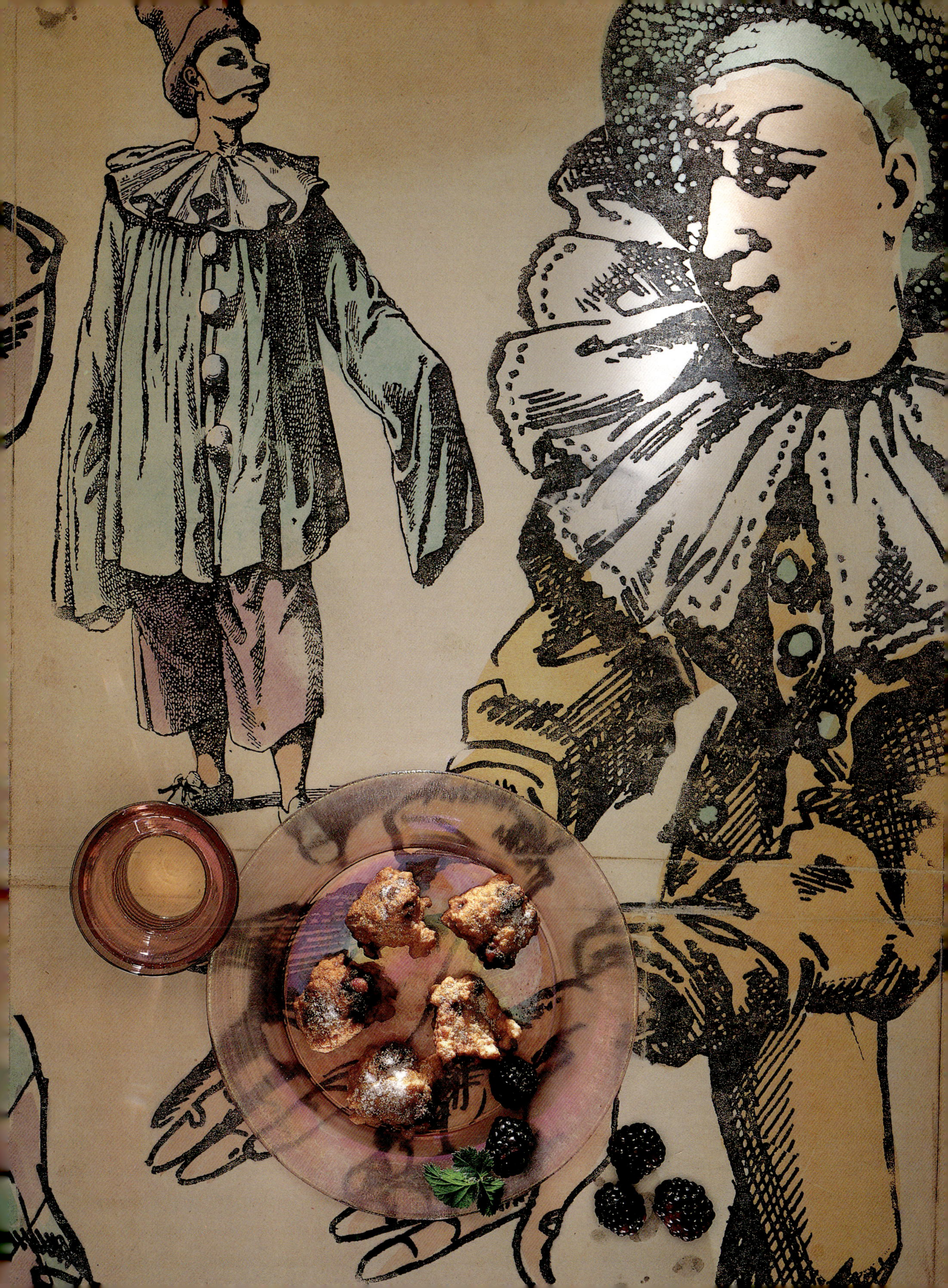

## CLASSIC ZABAGLIONE WITH MARSALA
### ZABAGLIONE CLASSICO AL MARSALA

*This version is the well-known classic dessert.*

**TIME 10-15 MINUTES**

4 egg yolks
4 tablespoons caster sugar
4 tablespoons Marsala

**1** Beat all the ingredients together lightly with a balloon whisk in the top half of a double boiler.

**2** Place the double boiler over the heat, making sure the water never touches the container with the egg mixture. Using an electric hand-held whisk, beat until pale yellow, light and fluffy, and the mixture leaves a thick trail when allowed to drop from the whisk. Make sure it holds soft peaks and is very glossy before you stop whisking. The mixture must be whisked sufficiently to prevent it separating when chilled.

**3** Pour into stemmed glasses and serve or chill until required.

## LIGHT ZABAGLIONE WITH PROSECCO
### ZABAGLIONE LEGGERO AL PROSECCO

*This is a very pale yellow version of the classic dessert. If you do not have a double boiler, use a large heatproof bowl set over a pan of simmering water.*

**TIME 10-15 MINUTES**

4 egg yolks
4 tablespoons Prosecco
4 tablespoons caster sugar

**1** Beat all the ingredients together with a balloon whisk in the top half of a double boiler.

**2** Place the double boiler over the heat, making sure the bowl does not touch the water. Using an electric whisk, beat the egg mixture until it leaves a trail when allowed to drop from the whisk. It should be really glossy and form soft peaks.

**3** Pour into stemmed wine glasses and serve at once or chill until required.

## SPICED ZABAGLIONE WITH RED WINE
### ZABAGLIONE ALLE SPEZIE CON IL VINO ROSSO

**TIME 10-15 MINUTES**

4 egg yolks
4 tablespoons medium-dry red wine
4 tablespoons caster sugar
large pinch ground cinnamon
large pinch ground ginger
large pinch ground nutmeg
large pinch ground cloves

**1** Beat all the ingredients together with a balloon whisk in the top half of a double boiler.

**2** Place over the heat, making sure the water never touches the container with the egg mixture. Using an electric whisk, beat until light and fluffy, and the mixture leaves a thick trail when allowed to drop from the whisk. It should be really glossy and form soft peaks.

**3** Pour into stemmed glasses and serve at once. This is best served at room temperature.

## PEARS WITH MASCARPONE

**MASCARPONE CON LE PERE**

**TIME 5 MINUTES**

4 ripe pears, peeled, cored and quartered
200 g/7 oz mascarpone cheese

1 Arrange the pear quarters in 4 small glass bowls.

2 Put the mascarpone in the centre of each bowl on top of the pears.

3 Serve immediately.

## STRAWBERRIES IN BALSAMIC VINEGAR

**FRAGOLE ALL'ACETO BALSAMICO**

*An unusual flavour combination, which actually works extremely well.*

**TIME 20 MINUTES**

500 g/1 lb strawberries
3-4 tablespoons balsamic vinegar
sugar to taste

1 Hull and wash the strawberries.

2 Put all the strawberries into a bowl, sprinkle with the vinegar and mix. Leave to stand for about 10 minutes.

3 Add sugar to taste, mix again and serve.

## GRAPES IN HONEY WITH BRANDY

**UVA AL MIELE CON COGNAC**

**TIME 5 MINUTES**

750 g/1½ lb white seedless grapes, washed, stalks removed
4 tablespoons runny honey
4 tablespoons brandy

1 Put all the grapes into a bowl.

2 Mix the honey and brandy together very thoroughly. Pour over the grapes and mix together with 2 spoons. Chill until required.

## PEACHES STUFFED WITH ALMONDS AND RICOTTA

**PESCHE CON LA RICOTTA E LE MANDORLE**

**TIME 10 MINUTES**

8 small peaches, stoned
100 g/4 oz fresh ricotta cheese
75 g/3 oz mixed blanched and unblanched almonds, coarsely chopped
2 tablespoons caster sugar
large pinch ground cinnamon

1 Make sure the peach halves are tidy and place them open side up on a pretty serving dish.

2 Mash the ricotta cheese with the other ingredients and fill the halved peaches with the mixture. Serve at once.

**OVERLEAF**
Above *Strawberries in balsamic vinegar*
Middle *Grapes in honey with brandy*
Bottom *Peaches stuffed with almonds and ricotta*

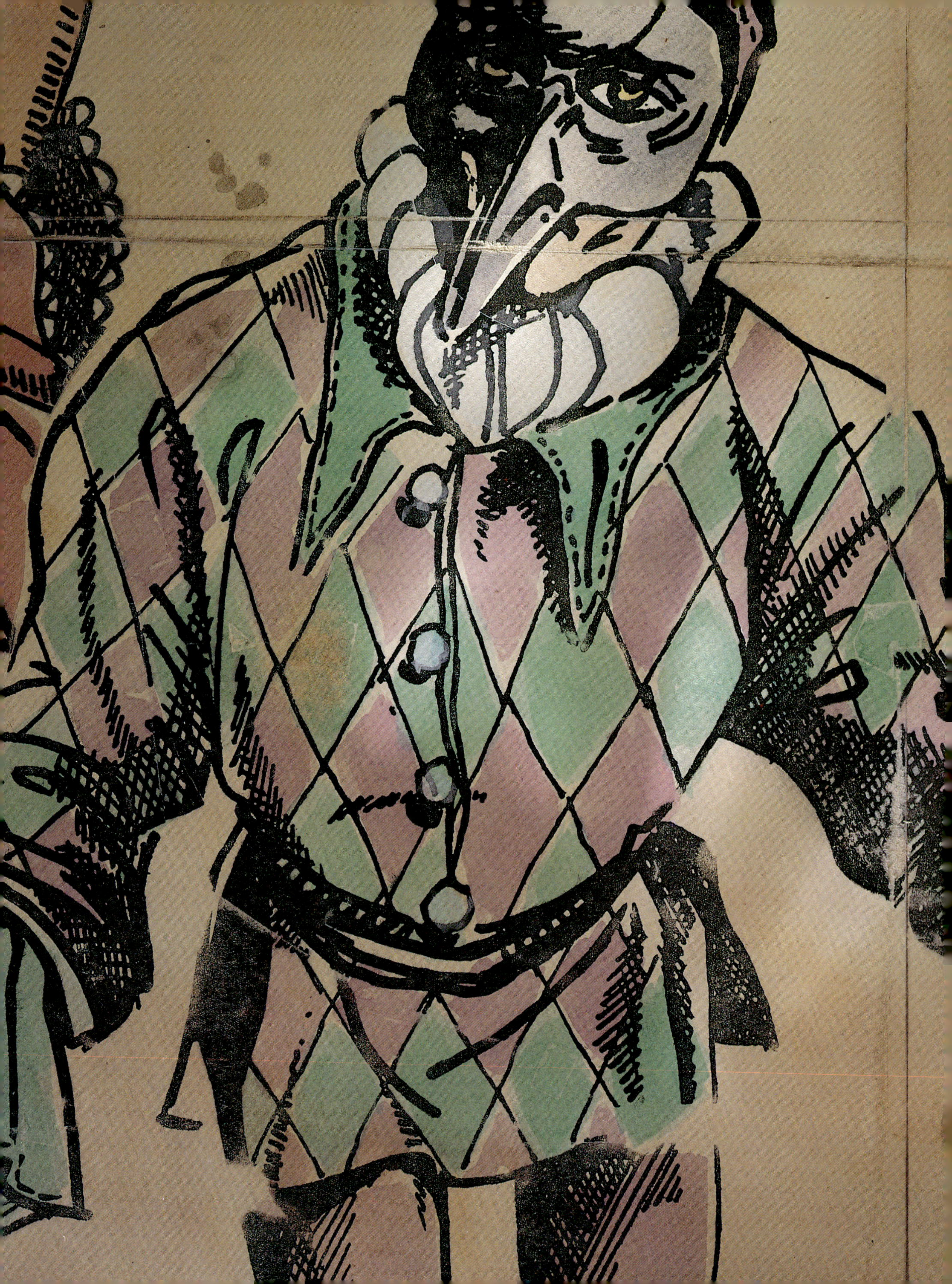

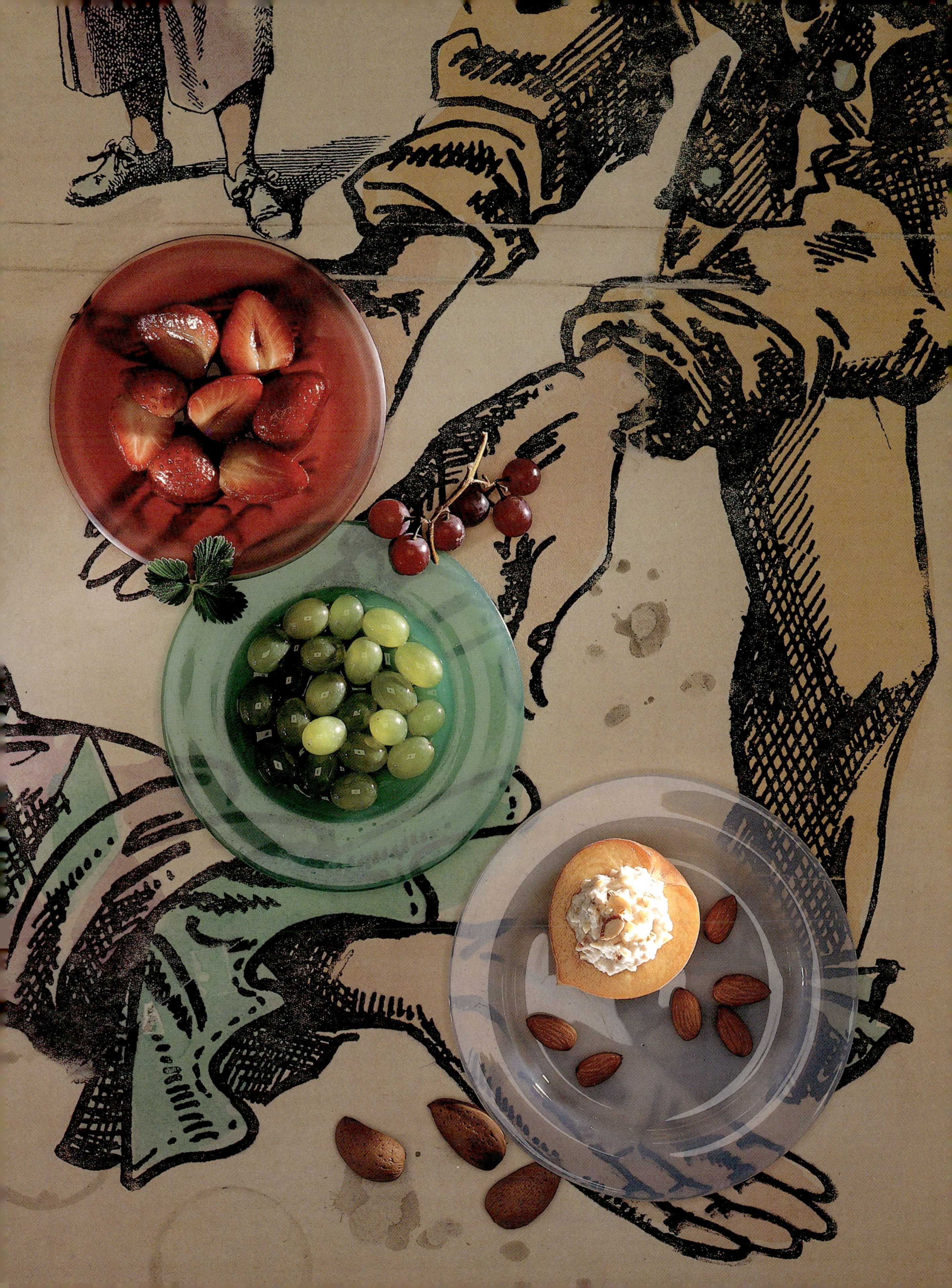

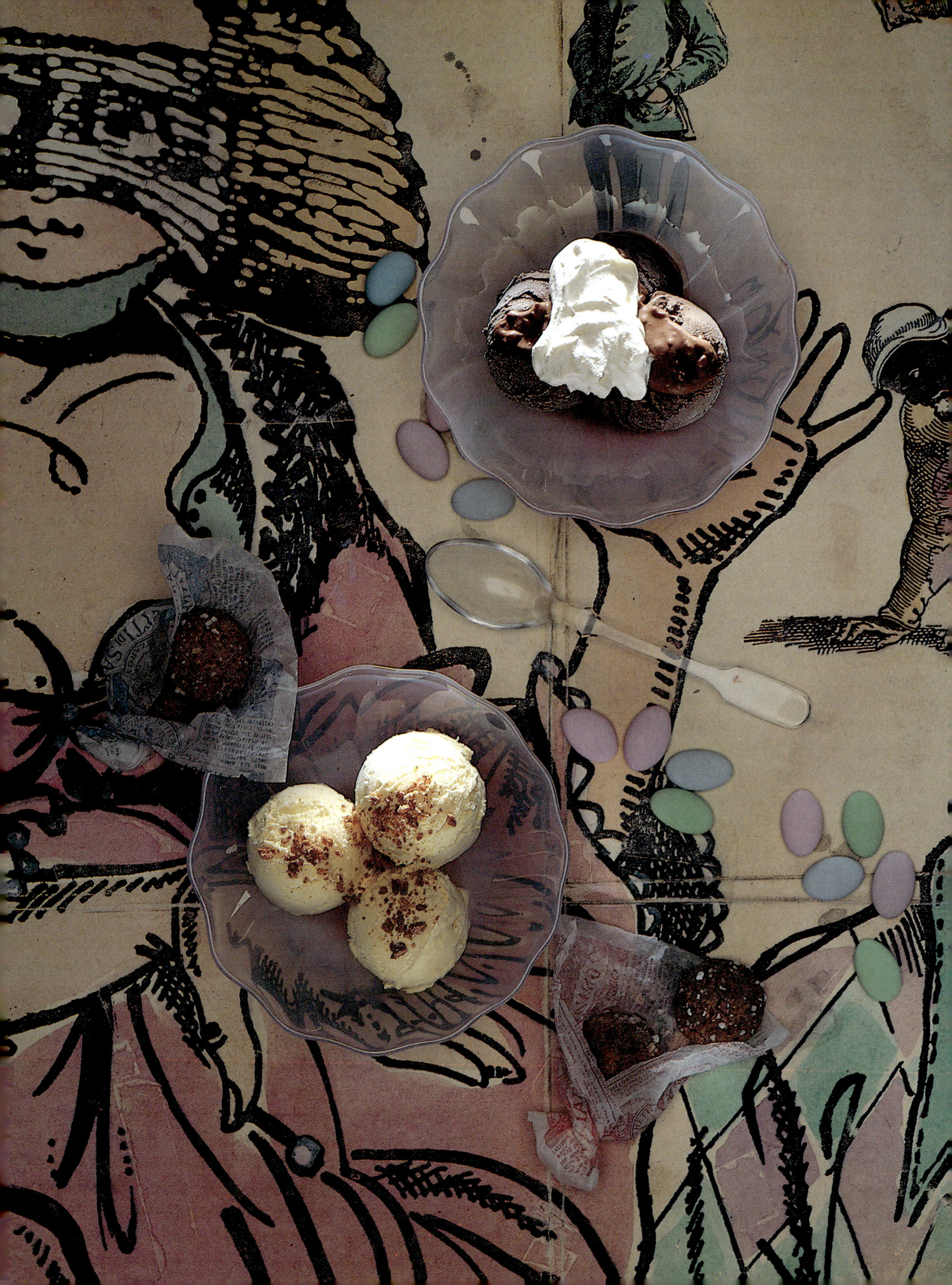

FRUIT AND DESSERTS 125

## CHOCOLATE ICE CREAM WITH BACI
### GELATO AL CIOCCOLATO CON CREMA DI BACI

*Perfect for chocaholics! Baci chocolates are walnut-sized, silver-wrapped milk chocolates with a hazelnut praline. The name means kiss, and the romance of the chocolates carries on to the little love notes tucked inside each wrapper. Baci are widely available, but if you can't get hold of them, use any hazelnut praline chocolate.*

**TIME 8 MINUTES**

**4 heaped tablespoons double cream**
**8 scoops dairy chocolate ice cream**
**8 Baci chocolates, melted**
**hazelnut biscuits, to serve**

**1** Whip the cream until stiff.

**2** Arrange 2 scoops of ice cream in each of 4 bowls or stemmed glasses.

**3** Pour over the melted Baci chocolates, cover with the cream and serve. Delicious when accompanied with hazelnut biscuits.

## ICE CREAM DROWNED IN AMARETTO
### AFFOGATO AL AMARETTO

**TIME 5 MINUTES**

**8 scoops dairy vanilla ice cream**
**8 tablespoons Amaretto liqueur**
**6 amaretti biscuits, crushed coarsely**

**1** Put 2 scoops of ice cream in each of 4 sundae glasses or pretty bowls.

**2** Pour 2 tablespoons of the liqueur on top of each serving of ice cream.

**3** Sprinkle generously with the crushed amaretti biscuits and serve at once.

**Above** *Chocolate ice cream with Baci*
**Below** *Ice cream drowned in Amaretto*

# INDEX

Page numbers in *italic* refer to the illustrations

*affogato al Amaretto*, *124*, 125
*affogato al brandy*, 118
*affogato al caffè*, 114
anchovies, 13
   grilled red pepper and anchovy salad, 58
   peppers with garlic and anchovies, 43, *44*
   potato salad with red onions and anchovies, 58
apples: hot apple and Amaretto cups, 114
artichoke hearts, lettuce and, 50, *51*
asparagus risotto, *82*, 83
avocado: avocado, mozzarella and sun-dried tomato salad, 53, *55*
   conchiglie with avocado and ricotta sauce, 73, *74*
   raw spinach, prosciutto and avocado salad, 56, 57

bacon: pea and bacon risotto, 83
*bavette Milanesi al limone*, 72
beef: grilled steak with garlic and olive oil, *92*, 93
   minute steak with garlic and tomato, 86, *89*
   thinly sliced fillet of beef with rocket, 94
*bistecchina all'aglio e pomodoro*, 86, *89*
*bistecca alla griglia con aglio e olio*, *92*, 93
blackberry fritters, hot, 118, *119*
*bocconcini di fichi e salame*, 28
borlotti bean and prawn salad, 37, *38*
*braciolette d'agnello con il peperoncino*, 87
brandy, ice cream drowned in, 118
bread, 8
   bread, tuna and basil salad, 50, *51*
   bread with sun-dried tomatoes and rocket, 52
   Tuscan bread salad, 52
*bresaola con la cipollina*, 20
bresaola with spring onions, 20
broad bean and pecorino salad, 36, *38*
broccoli: pasta and broccoli with pine kernels and chilli, 69, *70*
*bruschetta con il Parmigiano*, 46
*bruschetta con pomodoro e cipolle rosse*, 34, *35*
bruschetta: bruschetta with melted Parmesan cheese, 46
   bruschetta with tomatoes and red onions, 34, *35*
butter bean and mock caviar salad, 37

*caprino alla griglia nelle foglie di vite*, 29
celeriac and prosciutto salad, 62
cheese, 9-12
cherry risotto, 77
chicken: chicken breasts with lemon and rosemary, 90
   meatballs on a bed of leaves, 87, *88*
chicken livers, 22
chilli peppers, 12
   clams with chilli on toasted ciabatta, 104
   lamb chops with chilli sauce, 87
   trout with chilli and olive oil, 101, *102*
chocolate ice cream with Baci, *124*, 125
clams with chilli on toasted ciabatta, 104
*code di salmone alla griglia col pesto*, 107, *109*
coffee: ice cream drowned in espresso, 114
*conchiglie con avocado e ricotta*, 73, *74*
conchiglie with avocado and ricotta sauce, 73, *74*
*coppe calde di mele e amaretti*, 114
courgette risotto with basil, 76
courgette risotto with basil, 76
*cozze all'aglio con il coriandolo fresco*, 101, *103*
*cozze in una maionese allo zafferano*, 100
*crema di Gorgonzola al pâté con il pane di noci*, 26
crostini: with chicken livers, 22
   with mascarpone and walnuts, 23
   mushroom, 22
   tomato and olive crostini with capers, 34, *35*
*crostini ai funghi*, 22
*crostini al mascarpone e noci*, 23
*crostini con pomodoro e olive e capperi*, 34, *35*
*crostini di fegatini*, 22
*cuori di lattuga e carciofini*, 50, *51*
dates, ricotta-stuffed, 20, *21*
*datteri ripieni di ricotta*, 20, *21*
dip, green olive and walnut, 26, *27*
duck: duck breasts with pine kernels, 95
   duck breasts with Sicilian orange sauce, 94, *96-7*

eggs: coddled eggs with prosciutto and Parmesan, 47
   eggs in red pepper sauce, *40*, 41

fennel and lemon risotto, 77, *79*
*fettuccine con ricotta, pesto e pomodori secchi*, 68
fettuccine with ricotta, pesto and sun-dried tomatoes, 68
*fichi con la panna e il maraschino*, 115, *116*
figs: fresh figs with maraschino and cream, 115, *116*
   salame and fig bites, 28
*filetti di sogliola con i funghi*, 104, *105*
*filetto affettato con la rucola*, 94
*fragole all'aceto balsamico*, 121, *123*
*frittelle di more*, 118, *119*
fritters, blackberry, 118
*fritto di gamberi e seppie al limone*, 107, *108*
fruit and desserts, 9, 111-25

*gelato al cioccolato con crema di Baci*, *124*, 125
grapes in honey with brandy, 121, *123*

ice cream: chocolate ice cream with Baci, *124*, 125
   ice cream drowned in Amaretto, *124*, 125

ice cream drowned in brandy, 118
ice cream drowned in espresso, 114
*insalata di fagioloni bianchi e caviale finto*, 37, *39*
*insalata di fave e pecorino*, 36, *38*
*insalata di funghetti e Parmigiano*, 59, *60*
*insalata di gamberetti e borlotti*, 37, *38*
*insalata di melone e rucola*, 53, *54*
*insalata di mozzarella con capperi e olive*, 42
*insalata di avocado, mozzarella e pomodori secchi*, 53, *55*
*insalata di mozzarella, pomodorini e rucola*, 63
*insalata di olive nere, limoni e porri*, 36
*insalata di pane, tonno e basilico*, 50, *51*
*insalata di peperoni rossi alla griglia con alici*, 58
*insalata di radicchio con Groviera*, 63
*insalata di radicchio con Groviera*, 63
*insalata di sedano rapa e prosciutto crudo*, 62
*insalata di spinaci crudi col prosciutto crudo e l'avocado*, 56, *57*
*insalata mista con provolone*, 62

lamb chops with chilli sauce, 87
leeks: black olive, lemon and leek salad, 36
leek and pumpkin risotto, 81
lemon: Milanese bavette with zesty lemon sauce, 72

lettuce and artichoke hearts, 50, *51*

mango: prosciutto with mango and papaya, 43, *45*
*mascarpone con le pere*, 121
meat, 8-9, 85-95
meatballs on a bed of leaves, 87, *88*
melon and rocket salad, 53, *54*
Milanese bavette with zesty lemon sauce, 72
minute steak with garlic and tomato, 86, *89*
mushrooms, 9
fillets of sole with oyster mushrooms, 104, *105*
mushroom and Parmesan salad, 59, *60*
mushroom crostini, 22
mushroom risotto, 76
red wine and mushroom risotto, 80
mussels: mussels in saffron mayonnaise, 100
mussels with garlic and coriander, 101, *103*

olive oil, 16
olives: black olive, lemon and leek salad, 36
green olive and walnut dip, 26, *27*
pasta with garlicky olive sauce, 73, *75*
oranges: duck breasts with Sicilian orange sauce, 94, *96-7*
orange risotto, 78, *79*
*orecchiette con rucola e pomodoro crudo*, 69, *71*
orecchiette with rocket and fresh tomato sauce, 69, *71*

*pacchettini di prosciutto*, 30, 31
pancetta: warm radicchio with pancetta and provolone, 59, *61*
*pane ciabatta con prosciutto crudo e pomodori secchi*, 46
*panzanella con i pomodori secchi e la rucola*, 52
papaya, prosciutto with mango and, 43, *45*
*pappardelle con spinaci e panna*, 66, *67*
*Parmigiano con le pere e le noci*, 23, *25*
pasta, 13-16, 65-73
pasta and broccoli with pine kernels and chilli, 69, *70*
pasta with garlicky olive sauce, 73, *75*
*see also individual types of pasta*
*pasta con salsa d'olive e aglio*, 73, *75*
*pasta e broccoli con pinoli e peperoncino*, 69, *70*
*patate in insalata con cipolle rosse e acciughe*, 58
pâté: Gorgonzola and pâté with walnut bread, 26
pea and bacon risotto, 83
peaches stuffed with almonds and ricotta, 121, *123*
pears: hot pears with creamy Gorgonzola, 115, *117*
Parmesan with pears and walnuts, 23, *25*
pears with mascarpone, 121
peas: pan-fried plaice with peas and cream, 106
*peperoni con aglio e alici*, 43, *44*

*peperoni e pomodori secchi con mozzarella*, 23, *24*
peppers: eggs in a red pepper sauce, *40*, 41
grilled red pepper and anchovy salad, 58
peppers and sun-dried tomatoes with grilled mozzarella, 23, *24*
peppers with garlic and anchovies, 43, *44*
*pere calde al Gorgonzola*, 115, *117*
*pesce spada alla griglia con olio d'oliva e limone*, 110, *111*
*pesche con la ricotta e le mandorle*, 121, *123*
pesto, 16
fettuccine with ricotta, pesto and sun-dried tomatoes, 68
grilled salmon with pesto, 107, *109*
*petti d'anatra con i pinoli*, 95
*petti d'anatra con salsa d'arance Siciliane*, 94, *96-7*
*petti di pollo col limone*, 90
*petti di tacchino con prosciutto e formaggio*, 90, *91*
pine nuts, 13
duck breasts with pine kernels, 95
plaice, pan-fried with peas and cream, 106
*platessa con i piselli e la panna*, 106
*polpettine con l'insalata*, 87, *88*
*pomodori alla griglia con capperi e maggiorana*, 28
*pomodorini a pera ripieni di tonno e olive*, 42
potato salad with red onions and anchovies, 58
prawns: borlotti bean and prawn salad, 37, *38*

deep-fried prawns and squid rings with lemon sauce, 107, *108*
prosciutto: celeriac and prosciutto salad, 62
coddled eggs with prosciutto and Parmesan, 47
prosciutto and balsamic vinegar rolls, 28
prosciutto parcels, *30*, 31
prosciutto with mango and papaya, 43, *45*
raw spinach, prosciutto and avocado salad, *56*, 57
sun-dried tomatoes and prosciutto on ciabatta, 46
turkey breasts with prosciutto and melted cheese, 90, *91*
*prosciutto con aceto balsamico*, 28
*prosciutto con mango e papaya*, 43, *45*
pumpkin and leek risotto, 81

radicchio: radicchio and cream risotto, 80
radicchio salad with Groviera, 63
warm radicchio with pancetta and provolone, 59, *61*
*risotto ai funghi al vino rosso*, 80
*risotto ai funghi*, 76
*risotto al radicchio e panna*, 80
*risotto all'arancia*, 78, *79*
*risotto con finocchi al limone*, 77, *79*
*risotto con i porri e la zucca*, 81
*risotto con zucchine al basilico*, 76
*risotto d'asparagi*, 82, *83*
*risotto di cigliege*, 77
*risotto di pisellini e pancetta*, 83

rocket: bread with sun-dried tomatoes and rocket, 52
melon and rocket salad, 53, *54*
mozzarella, cherry tomato and rocket salad, 63
orecchiette with rocket and fresh tomato sauce, 69, *71*
thinly sliced fillet of beef with rocket, 94

sage leaves, deep-fried, 29, *30*
salame and fig bites, 28
salmon: grilled salmon with pesto, 107, *109*
mini salmon steaks poached in Prosecco, 106
*salmone lessato nel Prosecco*, 106
*salvia fritta*, 29, *30*
*scaloppine di tacchino con vino bianco alle erbe miste*, 95
*scaloppine di vitello al Marsala*, 86
*scamorza alla griglia sulla ciabatta*, 47
*seppie con aglio e olio*, 100
sole: fillets of sole with oyster mushrooms, 104, *105*
*spaghettini con salsa di Gorgonzola e salvia*, 72
spaghettini with Gorgonzola and sage sauce, 72
spaghettini with sun-dried tomatoes and pecorino, 81
spinach: pappardelle with spinach and cream, 66, *67*
raw spinach, prosciutto and avocado salad, *56*, 57
squid: deep-fried prawns and squid rings with lemon sauce, 107, *108*
squid with garlic and olive oil, 100

strawberries in balsamic vinegar, 121, *123*
swordfish: grilled swordfish steaks with olive oil and lemon, 110, *111*

*tagliolini con mascarpone e noci*, 66
*tagliolini con Parmigiano, prezzemolo e panna*, 68
tagliolini with Parmesan, parsley and cream, 68
tagliolini with walnuts and mascarpone, 66
tomatoes, 16
avocado, mozzarella and sun-dried tomato salad, 53, *55*
bread with sun-dried tomatoes and rocket, 52
bruschetta with tomatoes and red onions, 34, *35*
fettuccine with ricotta, pesto and sun-dried tomatoes, 68
grilled tomatoes with capers and marjoram, 28
mozzarella, cherry tomato and rocket salad, 63
orecchiette with rocket and fresh tomato sauce, 69, *71*
peppers and sun-dried tomatoes with grilled mozzarella, 23, *24*
plum tomatoes stuffed with tuna and olives, 42
spaghettini with sun-dried tomatoes and pecorino, 81
sun-dried tomatoes and prosciutto on ciabatta, 46
tomato and olive crostini with capers, 34, *35*
Tuscan bread salad, 52
*trota con peperoncino e olio d'oliva*, 101, 102
trout with chilli and olive oil, 101, *102*
tuna: bread, tuna and basil salad, 50, *51*
plum tomatoes stuffed with tuna and olives, 42
turkey: turkey breasts with prosciutto and melted cheese, 90, *91*
turkey escalopes with white wine and herbs, 95
Tuscan bread salad, 52

*uova al forno con prosciutto crudo e Parmigiano*, 47
*uova con salsa di peperoni rossi*, 40, *41*
*uva al miele con cognac*, 121, *123*

veal scaloppine with Marsala, 86

zabaglione: classic zabaglione with Marsala, 120
light zabaglione with Prosecco, 120
spiced zabaglione with red wine, 120
*zabaglione alle spezie con il vino rosso*, 120
*zabaglione classico al Marsala*, 120
*zabaglione leggero al Prosecco*, 120

### ACKNOWLEDGMENTS

Valentina Harris would like to thank Anne Furniss and Louise Simpson for all their hard work, and Diana Skarbon, Bruce Williams and everybody else who had a part (however indirect) in putting the project together.

Conran Octopus would like to thank Carluccio's, 28 Neal Street, London WC2 for their help in supplying props.